Potsdamer : Bibliothek östliches Europa
: Kunst

The Potsdam : Central and Eastern Europe Series
: Art

Orellen/Ungurmuiža (LV)

Agnese Bergholde-Wolf

Adeliges Leben im Baltikum
Herrenhäuser in Estland und Lettland

The Life of the Baltic Nobility
Manor Houses in Estonia and Latvia

Herrenhaus Dickeln/Dikļi (LV). Das neobarocke Haus wurde in den 1890er Jahren im Auftrag der Familie von Wolff gebaut. Heute wird das 2003 rekonstruierte Gebäude als Hotel genutzt, das zudem den im heutigen Lettland größten Bestand historischer und funktionstüchtiger Kachelöfen aus anderen Herrenhäusern und Stadtwohnhäusern von Riga versammelt.

Dikļi manor (Dickeln, LV). This neo-baroque house was built in the 1890s for the von Wolff family. After reconstruction in 2003 it is now used as a hotel and also houses Latvia's largest collection of historic (and still operational) tiled stoves from other country houses and town residences in Riga.

Inhalt • Contents

Vorwort • Preface   7
Das Baltikum. Kurze Geschichte der Region • The Baltic Region. A Short History   10
Baltische Gutshöfe. Adelige Lebensform • Baltic Estates. Life-Style of the Nobiliy   14

Herrenhäuser: Architektur und Ausstattung • Manor Houses: Architecture and Furnishings
Festes Haus, Stenhus. Frühe baltische Herrensitze • Fortified Stone Houses. Early Baltic Manor Houses   18
Barock im Baltikum. Herrenhäuser im 18. Jahrhundert • Baroque in the Baltic Region. 18th Century Manor Houses   24
Schlösser auf dem Land. Im Dienst der Herrscher • Country Residences. In the Ruler's Service   30
Zeitalter der Neo-Stile. Herrenhäuser im 19. Jahrhundert • An Age of Neo-Styles. 19th Century Manor Houses   36
Von Hütte bis Musenhof. Zur Ausstattung der Herrenhäuser • From Cottage to Court of the Muses. Furnishings in Manor Houses   42

Leben auf dem Gutshof • Life on a Manorial Estate
Ensemble mit Garten. Der traditionelle Gutshof • Manor with Garden. The Traditional Estate   50
Natur und Technik. Modernisierung der Gutsanlage • Nature and Technology. Modernisation of Estate Infrastructure   56
Von Rang und Stand. Grundbesitz und Selbstverständnis • Ranking and Status. Landed Property and Self-Image   62
Bauern und Bedienstete. Arbeit auf dem Gutshof • Peasants and Servants. Work on the Estate   68
Selbstsicht und Fremdsicht. Gutsbewohner im Bild • Seen by Oneself and by Others. Depictions of Estate-Dwellers   72

Geschichte der Gutshöfe nach 1900 • Estates viewed historically since 1900
Entbrannter Zorn. Gutshöfe in Revolution und Krieg • Eruption of Rage. Manor Houses during Revolution and War   80
Baltische Tragödie. Das Ende der Gutsherrschaft • Baltic Tragedy. The End of Lords of the Manor   86
Ungeliebtes Erbe. Herrenhäuser zur Sowjetzeit • Unloved Inheritance. Manor Houses Under Soviet Rule   92
Engagement für den Erhalt. Baltische Herrenhäuser heute • Commitment to Conservation. Baltic Manor Houses Today   98

Anhang • Appendix
Ausgewählte Literatur • Selected Bibliography   106
Über die Autorin • About the Author   107
Abbildungsnachweis • Illustration Credits   108

Vorwort

Anliegen des vorliegenden Buches ist es, anhand ausgewählter Beispiele eine Einführung in die Geschichte der Herrenhäuser und Gutsanlagen im historischen Baltikum zu geben. Während heute unter »Baltikum« im Allgemeinen die drei Staaten Estland, Lettland und Litauen verstanden werden, bezog sich dieser Begriff im historischen Verständnis auf das ehemalige Herrschaftsgebiet des Deutschen Ordens bzw. auf die vormaligen Ostseeprovinzen des Russischen Reichs Estland, Livland und Kurland – also im Wesentlichen auf das Territorium der heutigen Staaten Estland und Lettland, die auch den Gegenstand dieser Darstellung bilden.

In beiden Ländern wurde die Landwirtschaft über Jahrhunderte von der Gutsherrschaft bestimmt, die in den Händen der adeligen Oberschicht überwiegend deutscher Herkunft lag. Deren Vorfahren waren meist im Dienste der Ordensritter vor allem aus Norddeutschland und Westfalen ins Land gekommen und hatten Landbesitz erhalten. Sie konnten ihre führende Stellung und ihre Rechtstitel nach dem Zerfall des Ordensstaates sowohl unter polnisch-litauischer als auch unter schwedischer und schließlich unter russischer Herrschaft wahren. Mit dem Entstehen der Nationalstaaten Estland und Lettland am Ende des Ersten Weltkriegs und mit den Agrarreformen in beiden Ländern 1919/1920 endete die wirtschaftliche und politische Vorrangstellung des deutschbaltischen Adels. Die Zweiteilung des Gebietes nach Sprachgrenzen bedeutete einen radikalen Bruch mit der bisherigen territorialen Ordnung und der von

◀ Herrenhaus Münkenhof/Muuga manor (EE, s. S. 67)

Preface

This book sets out to provide – by way of selective exemplifications – an introduction to the history of manor houses and the accompanying estates in the historic Baltic area. Today the »Baltic« is generally comprehended as comprising the three states of Estonia, Latvia, and Lithuania, but viewed historically this term is used for the area formerly ruled by the Teutonic Order, later the Baltic provinces of the Russian Empire. In other words to a large extent the territory of today's Estonia and Latvia which are the subject of this presentation.

In both countries agriculture was for centuries determined by manorial estates, which were mainly owned by an aristocratic upper class of predominantly German origin. Its forefathers mostly came from Northern Germany and Westphalia in the service of knightly orders and were granted land in this area. They managed to maintain their leading position and their legal rights after disintegration of the state dominated by the Teutonic Order and also later under Polish-Lithuanian, Swedish, and finally Russian rule. With the coming into existence of the nation states of Estonia and Latvia at the end of the First World War and the agricultural reforms of 1919/1920 in both countries the economic and political pre-eminence of the Baltic-German aristocracy came to an end. Division of this territory in accordance with linguistic frontiers signified a radical break with previous territorial organisation and the region's cultural tradition essentially shaped by Baltic Germans. Viewed in the light of that background, joint presentation of the history and

◀ Muuga manor (Münkenhof, EE, see p. 67)

Marmorsaal im Herrenhaus Lappier/Ozolmuiža (LV, s. a. S. 72 f., 90), Ende des 18. Jahrhunderts. Foto 1914

Marble hall in the Ozolmuiža Manor (Lappier, LV, see also pp. 72 f., 90), late 18th century. Photo 1914

den Deutschbalten wesentlich geprägten kulturellen Tradition der Region. Um die baltischen Herrenhäuser und Gutsanlagen vorzustellen, ist es vor diesem Hintergrund sinnvoll, deren Entwicklung und Geschichte in den heutigen Staaten Estland und Lettland gemeinsam zu betrachten.

Das Buch ist ein gemeinsames Projekt des Deutschen Kulturforums östliches Europa und des Herder-Instituts für historische Ostmitteleuropaforschung – Institut der Leibniz-Gemeinschaft. Es ist angelehnt an die gleichnamige Wanderausstellung, die ebenfalls von beiden Einrichtungen erstellt wurde. Beide Institutionen befassen sich mit dem kulturhistorischen Erbe in jenen Regionen des östlichen Europa, in denen einst Deutsche lebten oder heute noch leben. Während das Herder-Institut dabei wissenschaftlich ausgerichtet ist, wendet sich das Kulturforum mit seinen Veranstaltungen und Publikationen an eine breite Öffentlichkeit.

Der überwiegende Teil des historischen Fotomaterials befindet sich im Besitz des Herder-Instituts. Dazu gehört die Fotosammlung von Baron Wolff-Lettien, die etwa 4 000 Negative umfasst. Die ursprünglich vermutlich bedeutend größere Dokumentation entstand in den 1920/30er Jahren. Viele der aktuellen Aufnahmen von Herrenhäusern und Gebäuden der Gutsensembles in Lettland sind der Fotosammlung des lettischen Fotografen Vitolds Mašnovskis entnommen, die ebenfalls im Bildarchiv des Herder-Instituts aufbewahrt wird. Zahlreiche Aufnahmen des heutigen Zustands gutsherrschaftlicher Gebäude in Estland und Lettland stammen von dem Fotografen Thomas Helms aus Schwerin.

Harald Roth
Direktor des Deutschen Kulturforums östliches Europa
Director of the German Cultural Forum for Central and Eastern Europe

development of Baltic manor houses and manorial estates in what are today the two states of Estonia and Latvia is an appropriate approach.

This book was jointly conceived by the German Cultural Forum for Central and Eastern Europe and the Herder Institute for Historical Research on East Central Europe – Institute of the Leibniz Association. It is based on the travelling exhibition of the same name, which was also created by the two institutions. Both are concerned with the cultural and historical legacy in those regions of Central and Eastern Europe where Germans used to, and still do, live. The Herder Institute pursues a more scholarly emphasis whereas the Cultural Forum directs its events and publications towards a general public.

Most of the historic photographs in the exhibition are owned by the Herder Institute. This material includes Baron Wolff-Lettien's collection of around 4 000 negatives. This originally probably much more extensive documentation was accumulated in the 1920s and 1930s. Many of the contemporary photographs of manor houses and estate buildings in Latvia come from the collection assembled by Vitolds Mašnovskis, the Latvian photographer, and these are also part of the Herder Institute's photographic archive. Many images of the present state of manorial buildings in Estonia and Latvia are the work of Thomas Helms from Schwerin.

Peter Haslinger
Direktor des Herder-Instituts für historische Ostmitteleuropaforschung, Institut der Leibniz Gemeinschaft
Director of the Herder Institute for Historical Research on East Central Europe – Institute of the Leibniz Association

Das Baltikum
Kurze Geschichte der Region

Heute bezeichnet man mit dem Begriff Baltikum drei Länder an der Ostsee, von Norden nach Süden sind es Estland, Lettland und Litauen. Der Begriff wurde im 19. Jahrhundert geprägt und bezog sich damals ausschließlich auf das ehemalige Herrschaftsgebiet des Schwertbrüderordens später des Deutschen Ordens, also Alt-Livland. Es bestand bis Mitte des 16. Jahrhunderts und umfasst im Wesentlichen das Territorium der heutigen Staaten Estland und Lettland. Mit den Ordensrittern kamen deutsche Adelige ins Land, Kaufleute aus den deutschen und skandinavischen Ländern ließen sich in den Städten nieder. Sie bildeten auch unter polnisch-litauischer, schwedischer und russischer Oberhoheit bis Ende des 19. Jahrhunderts die Oberschicht, die deutschsprachig war und über besondere Rechte verfügte. Sie waren auch die ersten, die sich als Balten, später Deutschbalten bezeichneten.

Innere Auseinandersetzungen infolge der Reformation und der Einfall russischer Truppen unter Iwan IV. (den Schrecklichen) führten im 16. Jahrhundert zum Zusammenbruch der Ordensherrschaft. Einzelne Teile des Landes unterstellten sich Polen-Litauen, Dänemark oder Schweden oder wurden von diesen erobert. Im Laufe des

◂ Das Gut Viol/Vihula (EE). Das 1501 erstmals erwähnte Gut war seit Anfang des 19. Jahrhunderts im Besitz der Familie Schubert, die es auch nach der estnischen Bodenreform 1919 als Restgut bewirtschaftete. Das Herrenhaus und seine vielen Nebengebäude liegen malerisch am Ufer des Violschen/Mustoja Flusses. Nach dem Zweiten Weltkrieg war hier ein Pflegeheim untergebracht. Heute findet sich in der restaurierten Gutsanlage ein Spa-Hotel und ein Restaurant.

The Baltic Region
A Short Story

Today the concept of the *Baltic region* (Baltikum) refers to three countries around the Baltic sea: from north to south Estonia, Latvia, and Lithuania. This denomination dates back to the 19th century when it referred exclusively to the area which in the middle ages was ruled by the Livonian Brothers of the Sword and later by the Livonian Order, an autonomous branch of the Teutonic Order. Old Livonia existed until the mid-16th century and has essentially become the modern states of Estonia and Latvia. German nobility came to this territory together with the Livonian Brothers of the Sword, while merchants from German and Scandinavian countries settled in towns. Until the end of the 19th century they built up a German-speaking upper class based on special rights, later on confirmed under Polish-Lithuanian, Swedish, and then Russian domination. They were also the first people to call themselves Balts and later German Balts *(Deutschbalten)*.

Internal disputes following the Reformation and invasion by Russian troops under Ivan IV (known as the Terrible) led in the 16th century to collapse of the Livonian Order. Different parts of the country submitted to Poland-Lithuania, Denmark, or Sweden – or were conquered by them.

◂ Vihula ewstate (Viol, EE). First registered in 1501, this was owned by the Schubert family from the start of the 19th century. What was left of the estate after the 1919 Estonian land reform was also run by the family. The manor house and its many subsidiary buildings are picturesquely situated on the river Mustoja (Viol stream). After the Second World War a nursing home was housed here. Today the restored estate buildings have become a spa hotel and a restaurant.

17. Jahrhunderts gelangte ein Großteil des Gebietes an Schweden. Nach dem Großen Nordischen Krieg (1700–1721) fiel es an Russland, Kurland, das zunächst ein selbstständiges Herzogtum war, erst 1795. Die Landesteile Alt-Livlands waren nun »russische Ostsee-Provinzen«.

Die Entstehung der Nationalstaaten Estland und Lettland im frühen 20. Jahrhundert beendete die herausgehobene Stellung der deutschen Oberschicht endgültig. Im Zuge des Hitler-Stalin-Paktes wurden die Deutschbalten 1939/40 in die Region um Posen und nach Westpreußen umgesiedelt. Estland und Lettland wurden, nachdem sie zunächst von der Sowjetunion und anschließend von der Wehrmacht besetzt worden waren, nach dem Zweiten Weltkrieg zu Sowjetrepubliken. Seit 1990 sind beide wieder unabhängige Republiken.

Wenn im Folgenden von »Baltikum« und »baltisch« die Rede ist, beziehen sich die Begriffe auf das Gebiet der heutigen Staaten Estland und Lettland. Synonym wird auch der Begriff Alt-Livland verwendet.

During the 17th century most of this area came under Swedish domination. After the Great Northern War (1700–1721) this succumbed to Russia – except for Courland, initially an independent Duchy, as late as 1795. The areas constituting Old Livonia were now »Baltic governorates of the Russian Empire«.

The coming into existence in the early 20th century of the nation-states of Estonia and Latvia put an end to the German upper class's special status. The German-Soviet Non-Aggression Pact led to German Balts being resettled around Poznań (Posen) and in West Prussia in 1939/40. After having been occupied first by the Soviet Union and then by the German Wehrmacht, after the Second World War Estonia and Latvia became Soviet Republics. Since 1990 both Estonia and Latvia are once again independent republics.

When the term »Baltic region« and »Baltic« are used in what follows this refers to the area consisting of today's states of Estonia and Latvia. Old Livonia is sometimes also used as a synonym.

▶ Die Zeichnung des Gutshofs Kunda (EE), enthalten in der Reisebeschreibung (1647) von Adam Olearius (1599–1671), ist die älteste Ansicht eines baltischen Gutshofs.

▶ This drawing of Kunda manor (EE) – in Adam Olearius's (1599–1671) account of a journey in 1647 – is the oldest view of a Baltic manor house.

Ansicht von Schloss Dondangen/Dundaga (LV, s. a. S. 84). Aquarell, Postkarte vor 1945. Die Burg Donedange wurde Mitte des 13. Jahrhunderts vom Deutschen Orden errichtet und ab dem 17. Jahrhundert nach den Erfordernissen eines Herrenhauses umgebaut. Durch Erbschaft gelangte das Rittergut Anfang des 18. Jahrhunderts in den Besitz der Familie Osten-Sacken. Anfang des 20. Jahrhunderts war es mit etwa 70 000 Hektar eines der größten Gutshöfe im Baltikum.

View of the residence at Dundaga (Dondangen, LV, see also p. 84), watercolour, postcard before 1945. Donedange castle was built by the Teutonic Order in the mid-13th century, and from the 17th century onwards converted to meet the requirements of a gentleman's residence. At the beginning of the 18th century this manor house was inherited by the Osten-Sacken family. By 1900 it was of the largest estates in the Baltic with around 70 000 hectares.

Baltische Gutshöfe
Adelige Lebensform

Baltische Herrenhäuser, erbaut, bewohnt und bewirtschaftet von der adligen Oberschicht meist deutscher, aber auch schwedischer, polnischer und russischer Herkunft, prägen den ländlichen Raum des heutigen Estland und Lettland bis ins frühe 20. Jahrhundert. Das Herrenhaus als Wohnort der Grundbesitzer war der zentrale und oft architektonisch am aufwendigsten gestaltete Teil eines Gutshofs. Dieser stellte eine Lebensform dar, in der Wohnen und Arbeiten eine räumliche Einheit bildeten. Dem deutschbaltischen Adel gehörten einige Hundert Familien an, die bis zu siebzig Prozent der Landfläche in Alt-Livland besaßen und damit auch wirtschaftliche und politische Macht ausübten. Seit dem Mittelalter organisierten sie sich korporativ in der Livländischen, Estländischen, Kurländischen und Öselschen Ritterschaft, benannt nach den vier Landesteilen Alt-Livlands. Im 17. Jahrhundert wurden auch Begünstigte der damaligen Landesherren zu Gutsbesitzern: in den nördlichen Regionen Mitglieder des schwedischen, in den südlichen Regionen entsprechend des polnischen Adels, ab dem 18. Jahrhundert auch Angehörige der russischen Aristokratie. Neben den mehrheitlich adeligen Rittergütern gab es im Baltikum auch weitere Güterformen, zum Beispiel Staatseigentum (Domänen), Stadtgüter (Patrimonialgüter) oder Besitz der Ritterschaften sowie zahlreiche Pastorate (mit einer Pfarrstelle verbundener Besitz) – insgesamt etwa 2 000 Güter. Die größten Güter konnten ein Ausmaß von mehreren Tausend Hektar haben mit ebenso vielen Bewohnern. Der Mindestumfang für ein Rittergut waren 900 Lofstellen, umgerechnet 328 Hektar.

Baltic Estates
Life-Style of the Nobility

Baltic manor houses were mainly built, inhabited, and run by the aristocratic upper class, mostly of German origin but also including nobles from Sweden, Poland, and Russia. They made their mark on the rural landscapes of today's Estonia and Latvia until the early 20th century. The manor house as landowner's residence was the central and often architecturally most extravagant element in an estate. This represented a way of life where living and working constituted a spatial unity. The German Baltic nobility comprised several hundred families who owned up to 70% of the land area in Old Livonia, and thus also wielded economic and political power. From the Middle Ages they were organised in the Baltic Noble Corporations of Saaremaa (Oesel), Estonia, Livonia, and Courland, named after the four regions of Old Livonia. In the 17th century protégés of the different sovereigns became landowners – in the north members of the Swedish aristocracy, in the south of the Polish nobility, joined from the 18th century by Russians. Alongside manors there were also other forms of ownership in the Baltic area: state-owned domains, city patrimony, estates held by Baltic Noble Corporations, and many parsonages together with parish land – in all around 2 000 properties. The largest of these estates could entail several thousand hectares with just as many inhabitants. The smallest manor house had 900 lofstelles (328 hectares).

Herrenhäuser: Architektur und Ausstattung
Manor Houses: Architecture and Furnishings

Festes Haus, Stenhus
Frühe baltische Herrensitze

Zu den ältesten Herrenhäusern im Baltikum gehören einige bis heute erhaltene mittelalterliche Burgen, die nach dem Untergang des livländischen Ordensstaates seit dem späten 16. Jahrhundert zu neuzeitlichen Wohnsitzen und Residenzen umgebaut wurden. Massiven, wehrhaften Charakter hatten auch die neu in Stein errichteten Herrenhäuser des 16. und 17. Jahrhunderts. Allein auf dem Gebiet des heutigen Estland waren nach Einschätzung neuester Forschung ein Zehntel aller damaligen Herrensitze solche festen Häuser und Wohntürme. Doch die Mehrheit der durch Kriege um die Vorherrschaft im Ostseeraum sowie durch die schwedische Güterreduktion (seit 1629) wirtschaftlich geschwächten Gutsherren baute in dieser Zeit preisgünstig aus Holz. Eingeschossige Gebäude in Blockbauweise über längsrechteckigem Grundriss mit Reet- oder Strohdach waren weit verbreitet. Der mittig angelegte Mantelschornstein bestimmte die Struktur dieser Häuser, die Räume verteilten sich rechts und links davon. Im Unterschied zu Bauernhäusern besaßen die herrschaftlichen Häuser keine Stallungen und dienten ausschließlich als repräsentativer Wohnsitz. Mancher Giebel und manches Portal hob sich durch künstlerische Gestaltung hervor.

◀ Turmburg Wack/Vao (EE). Die Turmburg wurde 1986 umfassend restauriert und kann heute im Rahmen einer Führung besichtigt werden. Im Erdgeschoss informiert eine kleine Ausstellung über die Geschichte der Burg, das Gut und seine ehemaligen Besitzer.

Fortified Stone Houses
Early Baltic Manor Houses

Among the oldest manor houses in the Baltic region are a number of still existent mediaeval castles, which from the late 16th century, after the downfall of the Medieval Livonian state, were converted into updated places of residence. The dwellings built in stone during the 16th and 17th centuries were also solid fortified constructions. According to the most recent research estimates a tenth of all manor houses at that time in what is today Estonia were such massive buildings and residential towers. However, most lords of the manor had suffered economically from wars over dominance of the Baltic area and from Swedish reduction of landed estates (from 1629), and built less expensively in wood. There were many single-storey log constructions on a long rectangular ground-plan with a reed or straw roof. The clad chimney in the middle determined the structure of these houses with rooms to the right and left. Unlike farmhouses these manorial buildings served exclusively as prestigious dwellings without stables. Some artistically embellished gables and doorways are noteworthy.

◀ Vao tower (Wack, EE). This was comprehensively restored in 1986 and can be visited today as part of a guided tour. A small exhibition on the ground-floor provides information about the history of the tower, estate, and former owners.

Herrenhaus Alt-Isenhof/Purtse (EE). Das Steingebäude auf quadratischem Grundriss mit starken Mauern und wenigen Öffnungen stammt vermutlich aus dem 16. Jahrhundert und zeigt charakteristische Merkmale früher befestigter Wohnsitze.

Purtse manor house (Alt-Isenhof, EE). This square stone building with strong walls and few openings probably dates from the 16th century. It demonstrates characteristic features of early fortified dwellings.

Turmburg Wack/Vao (EE). Das viergeschossige Gebäude aus dem späten 14. oder frühen 15. Jahrhundert gehört zu den ältesten Wohnbauten in Alt-Livland. Der Name des festen Hauses geht auf die ursprüngliche Eigentümerfamilie Wack zurück.

Vao tower (Wack, EE). This four-storey building from the late 14th or early 15th century is one of the most ancient dwellings in Old Livonia. Its name comes from the original owners, the Wack family.

Festes Haus Groß-Stenden/Dižstende (LV). Das in Resten erhaltene Steinhaus wurde im Auftrag von Philipp von der Brüggen (gest. 1556) errichtet. Das Gut blieb fast 400 Jahre im Besitz der Familie von der Brüggen.

Remains of a stone house at Dižstende (Groß-Stenden, LV). This was built for Philipp von der Brüggen (d. 1556) whose descendants owned the estate for almost 400 years.

Das Gutsgebäude in Kabillen/Kabile (LV, s. a. S. 55) wurde im 17. Jahrhundert als Wohnhaus aus Backstein erbaut. Das untere Geschoss ist gewölbt und verfügt über einen Ofen. Eine Besonderheit ist der bauzeitliche Fliesenfußboden mit figürlichen Reliefs, in der Gutsarchitektur des Baltikums ein einmaliges Beispiel. Ursprünglich war das Gebäude rot gestrichen. Die Herkunft der bis heute überlieferten Bezeichnung als »Rehstall« ist unklar.

The estate building at Kabile (Kabillen, LV, see also p. 55) was built of brick in the 17th century as a dwelling. The lower storey is arched and contains a stove. The contemporaneous tiled floor with figurative patterns is unique in Baltic estate architecture. This building was originally painted red. The origin of the still surviving designation of »deer stall« is uncertain.

▶ Herrenhaus Sandel/Sandla (EE). Erst um die Mitte des 18. Jahrhunderts gebaut, ist das einfache Gebäude auf der estnischen Insel Ösel/Saaremaa ein Beispiel für die schlichten, altertümlichen Herrenhäuser auf längsrechteckigem Grundriss mit Strohdach. Foto vor 1926

▶ Sandla manor (Sandel, EE). This simple building was erected in the mid-18th century on the Estonian island of Saaremaa (Ösel). It exemplifies traditional manor houses with a rectangular ground-plan and a straw-roof. Photo before 1926

Barock im Baltikum
Herrenhäuser im 18. Jahrhundert

Die wirtschaftlich schwierige Lage nach dem Großen Nordischen Krieg (1700–1721) sowie das Verbot der Errichtung von Steingebäuden in ganz Russland während des Aufbaus von Sankt-Petersburg im frühen 18. Jahrhundert bewirkten, dass man auch im Baltikum weiterhin in Holz baute. So ließ der in russischen Diensten stehende Johann Balthasar von Campenhausen (1689–1758) in den 1730er Jahren sein herrschaftliches barockes Wohnhaus in Orellen/Ungurmuiža (LV) aus Holz errichten. Neu war die Verlegung des Mantelschornsteins an die Seite des Hauses, so dass die Räume hintereinander folgend eine Enfilade bildeten. Zur gleichen Zeit entstand das steinerne Wohnhaus der Familie von der Pahlen in Palms/Palmse (EE), dessen heutiges Aussehen auf einem Umbau in den Jahren 1782 bis 1785 beruht. Die durch Pilaster und Fenster klar gegliederte Fassade im barocken Stil ist an Vorbilder in Riga (LV) und Narwa/Narva (EE) angelehnt, die sich ihrerseits an der holländischen Architektur orientierten. Allgemein zeichneten sich barocke Herrenhäuser durch eine größere Geräumigkeit aus. Die ein- bis zweigeschossigen Gebäude mit wuchtig wirkendem Walm- oder Mansardendach wurden im Inneren über aufwendige Treppenanlagen erschlossen. Den Eingang in der Hausmitte akzentuierte oft ein Risalit mit Giebel.

 Mehrflügelige barocke Schlossbauten wie Katharinenthal/Kadriorg (EE), Ruhenthal/Rundāle (LV) und Mitau/Jelgava (LV) blieben Ausnahmen in Alt-Livland. Diese herrschaftlichen Residenzen der Landesherren wurden von italienischen Architekten mit Unterstützung des russischen Zarenhofs errichtet.

Baroque in the Baltic Region
18th Century Manor Houses

Both the difficult economic situation after the Great Northern War (1700–1721) and a ban throughout Russia on construction of stone buildings while St. Petersburg was being developed in the early 18th century led to perpetuation of wooden houses in the Baltic region. Johann Balthasar von Campenhausen (1689–1758), who was in Russian service during the 1730s, thus had his grand baroque residence at Ungurmuiža (Orellen, LV) constructed in wood. Putting the clad chimney at the side of the house, so that rooms could be interconnected, was an innovation. The von der Pahlen family's stone residence at Palmse (Palms, EE) was built at the same time but then modified between 1782 and 1785. The baroque facade, clearly structured with pilasters and windows, was influenced by buildings in Riga (LV) and Narva (Narwa, EE), which in turn took over elements from Dutch architecture. Baroque manor houses were in general characterised by greater spaciousness. In the interior these one or two-storey buildings with mighty hipped or mansard roofs often contained lavish staircases. The entrance at the centre of the house was often accentuated by a risalit with a triangular gable.

 Baroque stately homes with several wings – as at Kadriorg (Katharinental, EE), Rundāle (Ruhenthal, LV), and Jelgava (Mitau, LV) – remained exceptions in Old Livonia. These grand residences for the sovereign were created by Italian architects with support from the Russian Tsar's court.

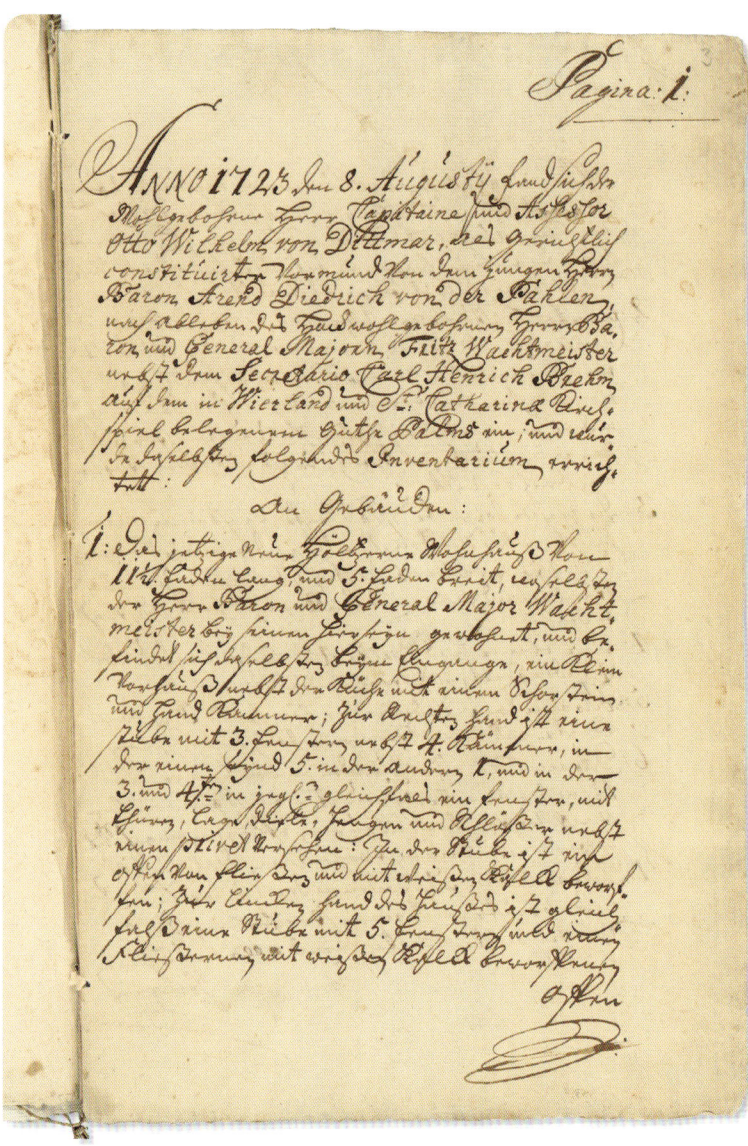

S. 24: Herrenhaus Palms/Palmse (EE, s. a. S. 50 f., 71). Das Gut Palms befand sich seit dem späten 17. Jahrhundert bis 1919 im Besitz der Familie von der Pahlen. In den 1930er Jahren wurde das Herrenhaus teilweise beschädigt. Fast die gesamte originale Einrichtung wurde im Zweiten Weltkrieg ausgelagert und zerstört. Aktuell beherbergt das Herrenhaus ein Museum mit Kopien früherer Einrichtungsgegenstände. Gutsgebäude werden als Hotel und Tagungsräume genutzt.

p. 24: Palmse manor (Palms, EE, see also pp. 50 f., 71). The Palmse estate was owned by the von der Pahlem family from the late 17th century until 1919. The manor house was partly damaged in the 1930s. During the Second World War almost all the original furnishings were moved and destroyed. Today the building has become a museum with copies of the original décor. Some of the former estate buildings are used as a hotel and conference rooms.

Inventar des Herrenhauses Palms/Palmse (EE) von 1723. Im Erbfall, bei Verkauf oder Umbau bzw. Wiederaufbau eines Gutes, wie in diesem Fall, wurden Inventare über den gesamten Besitz des Gutshofs erstellt. Im Verzeichnis aus Palms für das Jahr 1723, das 13 Seiten umfasst, sind Gebäude, Viktualien, Bettkleider und Vieh aufgeführt.

A 1723 inventory of Palmse manor house (Palms, EE). For inheritance, sale, or renovation/rebuilding, as in this case, inventories were drawn up of all of the estate's possessions. This 13-page listing included buildings, victuals, bed-furnishings, and livestock.

Das Herrenhaus Orellen/Ungurmuiža (LV, s. a. S. 2, 44) und die Alte Schule, Aquarell von Eugene Dücker, 1862. Das nie zerstörte Herrenhaus der Familie von Campenhausen ist bis heute der Mittelpunkt des über mehrere Generationen gestalteten, malerisch gelegenen Gutsensembles. Die Raumaufteilung im Inneren des Hauses wurde im Laufe der Zeit wenig verändert.

Die umfangreichen schriftlichen Überlieferungen im Familienarchiv, die vor allem von Siegfried von Vegesack (1888–1974) literarisch in Werken wie *Vorfahren und Nachkommen* eindrucksvoll verarbeitet wurden, vermitteln einen besonders guten Eindruck vom früheren Gutsleben auf Orellen. Heute wird das Gebäude multifunktional als Museum, Veranstaltungsort und Gästehaus genutzt.

Manor house at Ungurmuiža (Orellen, LV, see also pp. 2, 44) and the Old School, watercolor by Eugene Dücker, 1862. The residence of the von Campenhausen family has survived unscathed up to the present day as the centre-point of a picturesque ensemble of buildings constructed over several generations. The division of space inside the house was changed a little during that time.

The large number of manuscripts in the family archive, impressively utilised by Siegfried von Vegesack (1888–1974) in such literary works as *Vorfahren und Nachkommen* (»Ancestors and Descendants«), provide a particularly good impression of estate-life at Ungurmuiža in earlier times. Today the building serves a multi-functional purpose as museum, venue, and guest-house.

Allee zum Herrenhaus Selsau/Dzelzava (LV). Geradlinige oder geschwungene Alleen waren typische Zufahrtswege zu baltischen Gutshöfen. Eine Allee ist heute manchmal das einzige Überbleibsel eines Gutshofs und kann als solche ungeachtet jüngerer Bebauung zu beiden Seiten eindeutig identifiziert werden.

An alley leading to Dzelzava manor (Selsau, LV). Straight or winding alleys characterised access to Baltic estates. Today an alley may be all that is left of an estate but can be clearly identified despite younger building on both sides.

Herrenhaus Selsau/Dzelzava (LV). Wie viele andere wurde das barocke Herrenhaus aus der Mitte des 18. Jahrhunderts in den Unruhen von 1905 zerstört. Bald nach dem Wiederaufbau verließen die letzten Besitzer Selsau. Seit 1940 befindet sich im ehemaligen Herrenhaus eine Grundschule.

Dzelzava manor (Selsau, LV). This mid-18th century baroque house was destroyed, like many others, in the 1905 uprising. Soon after it had been rebuilt the last owners left Dzelzava. Since 1940 there has been a primary school in the former residence.

Schlösser auf dem Land
Im Dienst der Herrscher

Im 18. Jahrhundert orientierte sich der Adel im Baltikum auch an der Architektur am russischen Zarenhof. Vornehmlich Angehörige der vermögenderen Familien beauftragten in Russland bekannte und erfolgreiche Architekten mit dem Entwurf standesgemäßer Wohnsitze. Durch engste familiäre Verbindungen zum kurländischen Herzogshaus Biron und durch den Dienst am russischen Zarenhof genossen insbesondere die kurländischen Familien Medem und Lieven einen privilegierten Status. Das von zeitgenössischer englischer und italienischer Baukunst beeinflusste Gut Elley/Eleja (LV) der Familie Medem gilt als das erste rein klassizistische Schloss im historischen Livland. Ein mehrgeschossiger, mit Dreiecksgiebel bekrönter Säulenportikus war das bestimmende Gestaltungselement. Dieses herausragende Bauwerk wurde zum Maßstab für eine Vielzahl weiterer Herrensitze und Gutshäuser im heutigen Estland und Lettland. Wie ein Zwilling glich ihm das Herrenhaus Mesothen/Mežotne (LV). Es wurde für Charlotte von Lieven gebaut. Als Ausdruck des damals verbreiteten Ideals eines idyllischen Landlebens lagen die zwei- bis dreigeschossigen klassizistischen Häuser in ausgedehnten englischen Parklandschaften.

◂ Schloss Mesothen/Mežotne (LV, s. a. S. 42, 45, 58, 68). Charlotte von Lieven (1743–1828), die Erzieherin der Kinder der Zarin Katharina II., 1794 Hofdame und 1801 Oberhofmeisterin, wurde für ihre Verdienste in den Grafenstand und später in den erblichen Fürstenstand erhoben. Sie erhielt neben anderen Gütern Mesothen. In ihrem Auftrag erbaute Johann Georg Berlitz (1753–1837) 1821 das Schloss Mesothen nach einem Entwurf des russischen Hofarchitekten Giacomo Quarenghi (1744–1817). Es blieb bis zur Agrarreform 1920 im Besitz der Familie.

Country Residences
In the Ruler's Service

In the 18th century the Baltic landed gentry also sought orientation in Russian courtly architecture. It was mainly members of more affluent families who commissioned architects well-known and successful in Russia to design residences befitting their status. The Medem and Lieven families enjoyed a privileged position thanks to close family links with the ruling house of Biron in the Duchy of Courland and to their services on behalf of the Russian court. The Medem family's Eleja residence (Elley, LV), influenced by contemporary English and Italian architecture, is viewed as the first purely neoclassical residence in Old Livonia. The chief structural element was a multi-storey columned porch crowned with a triangular gable. This outstanding building set an example for many other manor houses in today's Estonia and Latvia. The residence at Mežotne (Mesothen, LV), built for Charlotte von Lieven, could be its twin. These two- or three-storey neoclassical buildings were surrounded by extensive park-like landscapes according with English fashion as an expression of the then current ideal of an idyllic rural existence.

◂ Mežotne residence (Mesothen, LV, see also pp. 42, 45, 58, 68). Charlotte von Lieven (1743–1828) was first governess to the children of the Tsarina Catherine II, and then appointed as lady-in-waiting in 1794 and Mistress of the Robes in 1801. Her services were rewarded by being made a countess and later a princess. Alongside other estates she was granted Mežotne where in 1821 Johann Georg Berlitz (1753–1837) built a grand residence designed by Giacomo Quarenghi (1744–1817), the Russian court architect. This remained in the family's possession until the 1920 agricultural reforms.

Herrenhaus Kolk/Kolga (EE). In die oberen Räume des palastartigen Hauses gelangt man über eine Treppe, deren Geländer die geschwungenen Initialen des Erbauers Karl Magnus Graf Stenbock (1725–1798) sowie die Jahreszahl 1768 schmücken.

Kolga manor (Kolk, EE). The upper rooms of this palace-like residence are reached by way of a staircase whose bannister is embellished with the florid initials of Karl Magnus Count Stenbock (1725–1798) and the date of the year 1768.

Herrenhaus Kolk/Kolga (EE). Es gehörte zu einem der ältesten, größten und reichsten Güter in der Ostseeprovinz Estland. Das heute noch bestehende repräsentative Herrenhaus wurde von 1765 bis 1768 für Karl Magnus Graf Stenbock errichtet. Sein jetziges Aussehen geht auf einen umfassenden Umbau um 1800 zurück. 1993 wurde es den ursprünglichen Eigentümern, der schwedischen Familie Stenbock, restituiert.

Kolga manor (Kolk, EE). This is part of one of the oldest, largest, and richest estates in the Baltic province Estonia. The prestigious dwelling was constructed between 1765 and 1768 for Karl Magnus Count Stenbock. Its present appearance dates back to extensive renovation around 1800. In 1993 it was returned to the original owners, the Stenbock family from Sweden.

Schloss Ratshof/Raadi (EE, s. a. S. 43, 45, 86). Die ältesten Gebäudeteile stammen aus dem 18. Jahrhundert, die jüngsten vom Anfang des 20. Jahrhunderts. Der Umbau um 1840 durch den in St. Petersburg und Odessa tätigen italienischen Architekten Francesco Carlo Boffo (1797–1867) im Stil der italienischen Renaissance gab dem Gebäude einen schlossartigen Charakter.

Raadi residence (Ratshof, EE, see also pp. 43, 45, 86). The oldest parts of this building date from the 18th century, and the most recent from the beginning of the 20th century. Italian architect Francesco Carlo Boffo (1797–1867), who worked in St. Petersburg and Odessa, converted this edifice around 1840 in the style of the Italian Renaissance, giving it a castle-like character.

Schloss Elley/Eleja (LV, s. a. S. 31, 81) wurde von 1806 bis 1809 von Johann Georg Berlitz (1753–1837) im Auftrag von Christoph Johann (Jeannot) Friedrich, Reichsgraf von Medem (1763–1838), nach dem Entwurf von Giacomo Quarenghi (1744–1817) errichtet, einem der bedeutendsten Architekten des späten 18. Jahrhunderts in Russland. Medem war kaiserlich-russischer Kammerherr und Bruder der Herzogin Dorothea von Kurland (1761–1821). Foto vor 1915

The Eleja (Elley, (LV, see also pp. 31, 81) large manor house was built between 1806 and 1809 by Johann Georg Berlitz (1753–1837) on behalf of Christoph Johann (Jeannot) Friedrich, Reichsgraf (Imperial Count) von Medem (1763–1838). This was based on plans by Giacomo Quarenghi (1744–1817), who was the leading architect of Neoclassicim in Imperial Russia. Medem was an Imperial Russian Chamberlain and brother of Duchess Dorothea von Kurland (1761–1821). Photo before 1915

Zeitalter der Neo-Stile
Herrenhäuser im 19. Jahrhundert

Die anhaltende wirtschaftliche und politische Stabilität der Region im 19. Jahrhundert fand ihren Niederschlag auch in der Ausgestaltung der Landsitze. In nur etwa hundert Jahren entstanden die meisten der heute noch erhaltenen Herrenhäuser. Die durch den Verkauf von eigenen Erzeugnissen wie Getreide, Branntwein, Milch- und Fleischerzeugnissen zu Wohlstand gekommenen Gutsbesitzer leisteten sich zeitgemäße Neubauten ihrer Wohnsitze. Namhafte einheimische und aus Deutschland stammende Architekten lieferten dafür Entwürfe in den verschiedenen Spielarten des Historismus. Der beliebteste Stil war die an der englischen Tudor-Architektur angelehnte Neogotik. Der ehemals kompakte, klar gegliederte Umriss der Häuser wurde aufgegeben.

Unterschiedlich große Türme, Türmchen und verschieden gestaltete Anbauten verliehen den Gebäuden einen verspielten, asymmetrischen Charakter. Anders als in den Städten fand die zeitlich darauffolgende Formensprache des Jugendstils in der traditionsgebundenen baltischen Adelsgesellschaft auf dem Lande nur wenig Anklang.

◀ Das Herrenhaus Alt-Autz/Vecauce (LV) ist eines der ersten neogotischen Herrenhäuser im Baltikum. Erbaut wurde es um 1845, vermutlich nach einem Entwurf des bekannten Berliner Architekten Friedrich August Stüler (1800–1865). Das Vorbild ist Schloss Babelsberg in Potsdam. Seit 1921 ist das Herrenhaus Sitz einer landwirtschaftlichen Lehr- und Forschungseinrichtung.

An Age of Neo-Styles
19th Century Manor Houses

The region's prolonged economic and political stability in the 19th century received expression in the designing of rural residences. Most of the still surviving manor houses came into existence within just about a hundred years. Estate owners who became affluent from selling the grain, distilled spirits, milk products, and meat they had produced commissioned new contemporary buildings to live in. Well-known local and German architects supplied plans for diverse historicist styles. The favourite was Neo-Gothic, based on English Tudor architecture. Houses' formerly compact and clearly structured ground-plan was then abandoned.

Towers big and small and variously conceived extensions endowed these buildings with a playful, asymmetrical character. When the language of Art Nouveau forms (Jugendstil) later made its way in urban areas the traditionally inclined Baltic rural noblemen were little impressed.

◀ Vecauce manor (Alt-Autz, LV) was one of the first neo-gothic dwellings in the Baltic region. It was built around 1845, probably based on plans by the well-known Berlin architect Friedrich August Stüler (1800–1865). Palace Babelsberg in Potsdam served as a model. Since 1921 the former manor has served as an agricultural college and research centre.

Schloss Stomersee/Stāmeriena (LV, s. a. S. 83). Mit dem Stammsitz der Familie von Wolff im Stil der Neorenaissance ist der Name des italienischen Schriftstellers Giuseppe Tomasi di Lampedusa (1896–1957), Autor des berühmten Romans *Der Leopard (Il Gattopardo),* verbunden. Der Ehemann der Psychoanalytikerin Alexandra von Wolff (1894–1982) hielt sich mehrmals in Stomersee auf.

Stāmeriena manor house (Stomersee, LV, see also p. 83). Giuseppe Tomasi di Lampedusa (1896–1957), Italian author of the celebrated novel *The Leopard (Il Gattopardo),* is linked with this ancestral seat of the von Wolff family, built in a Neo-Renaissance style. Lampedusa, husband of psychoanalyst Alexandra von Wolff (1894–1982), stayed at Stomersee several times.

Das Schloss Allatzkiwwi/Alatskivi (EE) wurde im Auftrag von Arved Freiherr Nolcken 1880 bis 1885 in Anlehnung an das Königsschloss Balmoral in Schottland erbaut. Das neogotische Herrenhaus liegt unweit des großen Peipus-Sees und beherbergt heute ein Museum. Aus Allatzkiwwi haben sich mehrere Hundert Einrichtungsgegenstände sowie umfangreiches Schrift- und Fotomaterial erhalten.

The large manor house at Alatskivi (Allatzkiwwi, EE) was built for Arved Baron Nolcken between 1880 and 1885, inspired by the royal residence at Balmoral in Scotland. This neo-gothic building is not far from Lake Peipus and today houses a museum. Several hundred pieces of furniture and many manuscripts and photos have been preserved.

Schloss Neu-Mocken/Jaunmokas (LV), erbaut 1885 von Wilhelm Bockslaff (1858–1945) im Auftrag von Georges Armitstead (1847–1912), dem Oberbürgermeister von Riga von 1901 bis 1912. Das ursprüngliche Jagdschloss ist heute ein Hotel, das auch ein Museum zur Geschichte des Hauses unterhält. Backstein als Baumaterial wurde bevorzugt in Südlivland bzw. auf dem Gebiet des heutigen Lettland genutzt, im Gouvernement Estland konnte man auf die heimischen Kalksteinvorkommen zurückgreifen.

Jaunmokas residence (Neu-Mocken, LV), built in 1885 by Wilhelm Bockslaff (1858–1945) on behalf of Georges Armitstead (1847–1912), Lord mayor of Riga from 1901 to 1912. The original hunting lodge is a hotel today, incorporating a museum on the house's history. Brick was the preferred building material in Southern Livonia and in today's Latvia. In the Baltic province Estonia local limestone was used.

▸ Salon im Schloss Groß-Autz/Lielauce (LV)
Die Inneneinrichtung auf dem Anfang des 20. Jahrhunderts entstandenen Foto stammt zum größten Teil aus der Zeit von 1830/1840.

▸ A salon in the Lielauce residence (Groß-Autz, LV).
The interior furnishings shown on this photo from the beginning of the 20th century largely date from around 1830/1840.

Von Hütte bis Musenhof
Zur Ausstattung der Herrenhäuser

Über die Ausstattung früher Herrenhäuser im historischen Livland wissen wir nur wenig. Die aus Kassel stammende und nach Asuppen/Aizupe (LV) eingeheiratete Freifrau Sophie von Hahn (1804–1863) stellte bei ihrer Schilderung der Lage in Kurland in den 1820er Jahren fest: »In dem herrschaftlichen Ameublement war alles auf das Minimum berechnet«. Ein anderes Mal war sie von »einer ansehnlichen, eleganten und komfortablen Wohnung« entzückt (*In Gutshäusern,* S. 167–174). Die Zitate zeigen die großen Unterschiede bezüglich der Einrichtung in den einzelnen baltischen Herrenhäusern. Erst der allgemeine Wohlstand der Gutsbesitzer in der zweiten Hälfte des 19. Jahrhunderts ermöglichte eine aufwendige bis reiche Ausstattung, in Einzelfällen mit Mobiliar und Kunstwerken von europäischem Rang. Aus der Verbindung von Kunstsinn und Vermögen ging die herausragende Sammlung der Familie von Liphart in Ratshof/Raadi (EE) bei Dorpat/Tartu hervor. Das mit Kunstschätzen reich ausgestattete Schloss war Treffpunkt von einheimischen wie ausländischen Künstlern, Musikern und Literaten, die von der Familie Liphart großzügig unterstützt wurden. Beim Brand des Hauses 1944 ging die Sammlung unwiederbringlich verloren. Ein Teil der großen und wertvollen Kunstsammlung der Familie Transehe-Roseneck auf Neu-Schwanenburg/Jaungulbene (LV) hat sich durch eine Schenkung der Familie im Jahr 1904 im Bestand des heutigen Lettischen Nationalen Kunstmuseums in Riga (*Latvijas Nacionālais mākslas muzejs*) erhalten. Auf ähnliche Weise gelangten Kunstgegenstände auch aus anderen Herrenhäusern in die heutigen Museen Estlands und Lettlands.

From Cottage to Court of the Muses
Furnishings in Manor Houses

We know little about furnishings of manor houses in Old Livonia. Baroness Sophie von Hahn (1804–1863) – who came from Kassel and married into a family at Aizupe (Asuppen, LV) – described the situation in the Courland of the 1820s: »Aristocratic furnishings were reduced to a minimum«. On another occasion she was delighted by »a handsome, elegant, and comfortable dwelling«. Those responses demonstrate the great differences in the furnishing of individual Baltic manor houses. Only the widespread affluence of the nobility in the second half of the 19th century made possible rich or even lavish embellishment of residences, sometimes with furniture and artworks of European importance. The outstanding collection assembled by the von Liphart family at Raadi (Ratshof, near Tartu/Dorpat, EE) was the outcome of an overlapping of artistic taste and money. This residence, richly endowed with artistic treasures, was a meeting-place for both local and foreign artists, musicians, and men of letters, who were generously supported by the Liphart family. When the house burned down in 1944 the collection was lost for ever. A part of the large and valuable art collection of the Transehe-Roseneck family from Jaungulbene (Neu-Schwanenburg, LV) was saved thanks to its donation in 1904 to what is today the Latvian National Museum of Art in Riga *(Latvijas Nacionālais mākslas muzejs)*. In a similar way art from other manor houses also ended up in contemporary Estonian and Latvian museums.

Herrenhaus Orellen/Ungurmuiža (LV, s. a. S. 2, 27). Die Ausmalung im Inneren führte der einheimische Maler Georg Dietrich Hinsch in den 1750/60er Jahren aus. Die bekanntesten Motive sind die lebensgroßen Grenadiere, die beiderseits des Schlafzimmers des Bauherrn Wache halten. Vermutlich erinnern sie an die Dienstzeit Johann Balthasar von Campenhausens (1689–1758) in der russischen Armee. In der baltischen dekorativen Malerei sind diese Darstellungen einmalig.

Manor house in Ungurmuiža (Orellen, LV, see also pp. 2, 27). The wall-paintings in the house were done in the 1750s/1760s by a local artist, Georg Dietrich Hinsch. The most celebrated motifs are two life-size grenadiers who keep watch on the two sides of the door leading to the lord of the manor's bedroom. They probably recall Johann Balthasar von Campenhausen's (1689–1758) service in the Russian army. These depictions are unique in Baltic decorative painting.

S. 42: Schloss Mesothen/Mežotne (LV, s. a. S. 30 f., 58, 68). Der um 1800 errichtete Kuppelsaal mit seinen Stuckornamenten und Malereien ist ein Meisterwerk ersten Ranges. Nach Beschädigungen während der beiden Weltkriege wurde das Gebäude immer wieder restauriert. Heute ist in den Räumen ein Hotel untergebracht.

p. 42: Mežotne residence (Mesothen, LV, see also pp. 30 f., 58, 68). The hall (built around 1800) with its cuppola, stucco decoration, and paintings is an outstanding masterpiece. After severe damage in both World Wars the building was time and again restored. Today it houses a hotel.

Schloss Ratshof/Raadi (EE, s. a. S. 34, 86). Das Schloss war seit 1751 im Besitz der Familie von Liphart, die es bis zur Bodenreform 1919 besaß. Das Herrenhaus wurde mehrfach umgestaltet und erweitert. 200 Gemälde weltbekannter italienischer, niederländischer und deutscher Maler, Grafiken, Skulpturen der italienischen Renaissance, Möbel und eine große Bibliothek wurden in entsprechend stilgerechten Räumen präsentiert. Von 1921 bis 1944 Sitz des Estnischen Nationalmuseums, ist das Haus heute eine Ruine. Foto vor 1944

Raadi manor house (Ratshof, EE, see also pp. 34, 86). This residence was owned by the von Liphart family from 1751 until land reform in 1919. It was refashioned and extended on many occasions. 200 paintings by world famous Italian, Dutch, and German painters, prints and sculpture from the Italian Renaissance, furniture, and a large library were displayed in rooms appropriately styled. The house served as the Estonian National Museum from 1921 to 1944, but today is a ruin. Photo before 1944

Herrenhaus Asuppen/Aizupe (LV, s. a. S. 75). Im Kabinett des im frühen 19. Jahrhundert erbauten Hauses der Familie von Hahn befand sich ein Teil der etwa 20 000 Bände umfassenden Bibliothek. An den von der Decke herabhängenden Stangen links im Bild wurden Karten, zumeist größere Flurkarten, zum Anschauen befestigt. Foto nach 1920

Aizupe manor house (Asuppen, LV, see also p. 75). Some of the 20 000 books in the library were displayed in a small study in the von Hahn family's dwelling, built in the early 19th century. Large field maps were attached to the bars hanging down from the ceiling. Photo after 1920

Herrenhaus Neu-Autz/Jaunauce (LV). Hinter den schlichten Außenfassaden des Herrenhauses liegt ein prächtiger, großräumiger Saal mit kassettierter Kuppel und Öfen im Empire-Stil. Einst schmückten den Raum Marmorskulpturen nach antiken Vorbildern, die die Eigentümerfamilie von der Ropp in der Werkstatt des bekannten dänischen Bildhauers Bertel Thorvaldsen (1770–1844) anfertigen ließ. Foto um 1910

Jaunauce manor (Neu-Autz, LV). Behind the building's simple external facade is a large and splendid room with a coffered cupola and empire-style stoves. This space was once adorned by marble sculptures based on models from classical antiquity, commissioned by the von der Ropp family from the workshop of Bertel Thorvaldsen (1770–1844), a well-known Danish sculptor. Photo about 1910

Leben auf dem Gutshof
Life on a Manorial Estate

Ensemble mit Garten
Der traditionelle Gutshof

Die Gebäude des Gutshofs konnten um eine Freifläche, einen rechteckigen, ovalen oder auch runden Hof gruppiert sein oder bildeten ein eigenständiges Ensemble etwas abseits vom Herrenhaus. Neben dem Herrenhaus umfasste der Gutshof Speicherräume und Ställe für Reit- und Arbeitstiere, aber auch Wohnräume für Bedienstete und verschiedene Wirtschaftsgebäude. Die räumliche Nähe zum Herrenhaus spiegelte sich im architektonisch und stilistisch einheitlichen Aussehen des engsten Hofensembles. Ställe und Getreidespeicher wurden mit Arkaden- oder Säulenreihen aufgewertet. Weitere Wirtschaftsgebäude wie Mühlen, Viehställe, Scheunen, Kornspeicher, Herbergen (Unterkünfte für Bedienstete), (Branntwein-)Brennereien oder Brauereien und Gasthäuser (Krüge) mit Pferdewechselstationen lagen im 19. Jahrhundert oftmals in Einzellage in einiger Entfernung vom Gutshof.

Seit dem späten 16. Jahrhundert gehörte im historischen Livland zudem ein Küchengarten mit Gemüse- und Kräuteranbau zum festen Bestandteil eines Gutshofs. Nach dem Großen Nordischen Krieg fand die Kunst der barocken Gartengestaltung auch hier großen Anklang. Die geometrische und symmetrische Anordnung von Gutsgebäuden und eine entsprechende bei der Anlage von Beeten, Baumreihen, Wegen und Sichtachsen in Gärten und Parks war bis ins späte 18. Jahrhundert hinein beliebt.

◁ Ansicht des Landguts Palms/Palmse (EE, s. a. S. 24 ff., 71). Anna von Gruenwaldt (1859–1913) schrieb in ihren 1914 erschienenen Erinnerungen über den mit Wegenetz, Kleinarchitekturen und Baumgruppen gestalteten weitläufigen Landschaftsgarten von Palms »[…] so Schönes gab es in der Welt nicht mehr«. (S. 17)

Manor with Garden
The Traditional Estate

Manor house buildings were grouped around a rectangular, oval, or circular courtyard, or constituted an autonomous ensemble some distance away from the residence. Alongside the residence were barns, stables, and stalls for working animals, together with accommodation for servants and various work-areas. Their closeness to the actual manor house was reflected in the unified architectural style of this ensemble. Stables and granaries were embellished with arches and columns. In the 19th century other work-areas such as mills, cattle stalls, barns, granaries, accommodation for farm-labourers, distilleries or breweries, and inns with facilities for changing horses were often some way from the manor itself.

In addition in Old Livonia from the late 16th century a kitchen garden for vegetables and herbs was an established feature. After the Great Northern War, the art of Baroque garden design was much cultivated also here. Geometrical and symmetrical ordering of estate buildings was frequent until the late 18th century, accompanied in gardens and parks by similarly formal flower beds, alleys of trees, paths, and sight lines.

◁ A view of the Palmse estate (Palms, EE, see also pp. 24 ff., 71). Anna von Gruenwaldt (1859–1913) wrote in her memoirs (published in 1914) about the network of paths, ornamental buildings, and groupings of trees in Palms' extensive landscape garden, declaring that »[…] such beauty won't ever exist again in our world«.

Wirtschaftshof von Gut Rogosinsky/Ruusmäe (EE). Die wehrhaft wirkende, kompakte Anlage, die vermutlich auf eine ältere Burg zurückgeht, umschließt einen rechteckigen Hof. Diese Form ermöglichte es, den Schmutz aus der Viehhaltung auf den Innenhof zu beschränken und so die Gutsumgebung sauber zu halten. Der repräsentative Torturm wurde im 19. Jahrhundert hinzugefügt.

The Ruusmäe estate's farmyard (Rogosinsky, EE). The compact and apparently defensible buildings, probably indicating an older fortress, enclose a rectangular courtyard. This made it possible to restrict muck and mud from cattle to the inner courtyard, and thus to keep the surroundings clean. The prestigious towered gate was added in the 19th century.

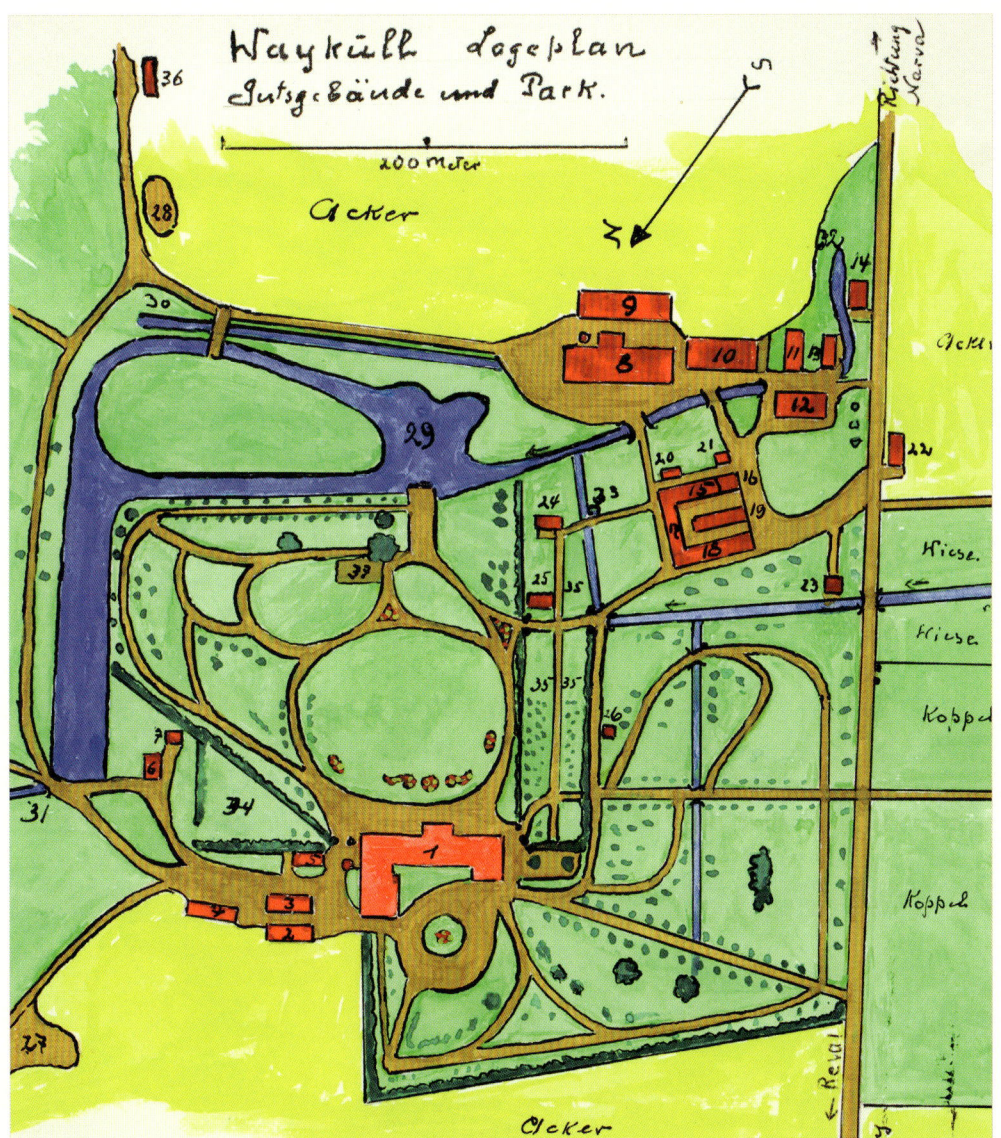

Lageplan der Gutsgebäude und des Parks von Wayküll/Vaeküla (EE). Das Gut war bis zur Bodenreform 1919 im Besitz der Familie von Schubert.

Plan of the estate buildings and park at Vaeküla (Wayküll, EE). This estate was owned by the von Schubert family until the 1919 land reform.

1 Herrenhaus/Manor house, **2** Kleete (Speicher)/Storage, **3** Kleete/Storage, **4** Kutschpferde, Wagenremise/Coach horses, coach-house, **5** Eiskeller/Cold-store, **6** Waschküche u. Sauna, Kutscherwohnung/Washhouse & sauna, coachman's accommodation, **7** Hühnerhaus/Chicken-house, **8** Brennerei/Distillery, **9** Mastochsenstall/Ox stall, **10** Kuhstall/Cow stall, **11** Jungviehstall/Calf stall, **12** »Herberge« = Arbeiterwohnung/Workers accommodation, **13** Schweinestall für die Arbeiter/Workers' pig-sty, **14** Schmiede/Smithy, **15** Maschinenschuppen/Machine shed, **16** Stallmeisterwohnung/Head groom's accommodation, **17** Geräteschuppen/Equipment shed, **18** Ackerpferdestall/Carthorse stall, **19** Offener Schuppen für Ackerwagen/Open shed for farm carts, **20** Schweinestall/Pig-sty, **21** Verwalterwohnung/Custodian's house, **22** Korndarre (zum Trocknen von Getreide)/Grain dryer, **23** Wohnung für Angestellte (erbaut für Hauslehrer)/Accommodation for staff (built for tutors), **24** Gärtnerwohnung/Gardeners house, **25** Gewächshaus/Greenhouse, **26** Gerätehaus im Park/Equipment building in the park, **27** Sandgrube/Sand pit, **28** Alter Kalkbruch/Old lime pit, **29** Künstlicher See/Artificial lake, **30** Klärgraben für Kartoffelwasser/Ditch for potato water, **31** Stauwehr für den See/Weir for the lake, **32** Quelle/Spring, **33** Quelle/Spring, **34** Wäschetrockenplatz/Laundry drying place, **35** Gemüse- und Obstgarten/Garden for vegetables and fruit, **36** Alte Scheune/Old barn, **37** Tennisplatz/Tennis court

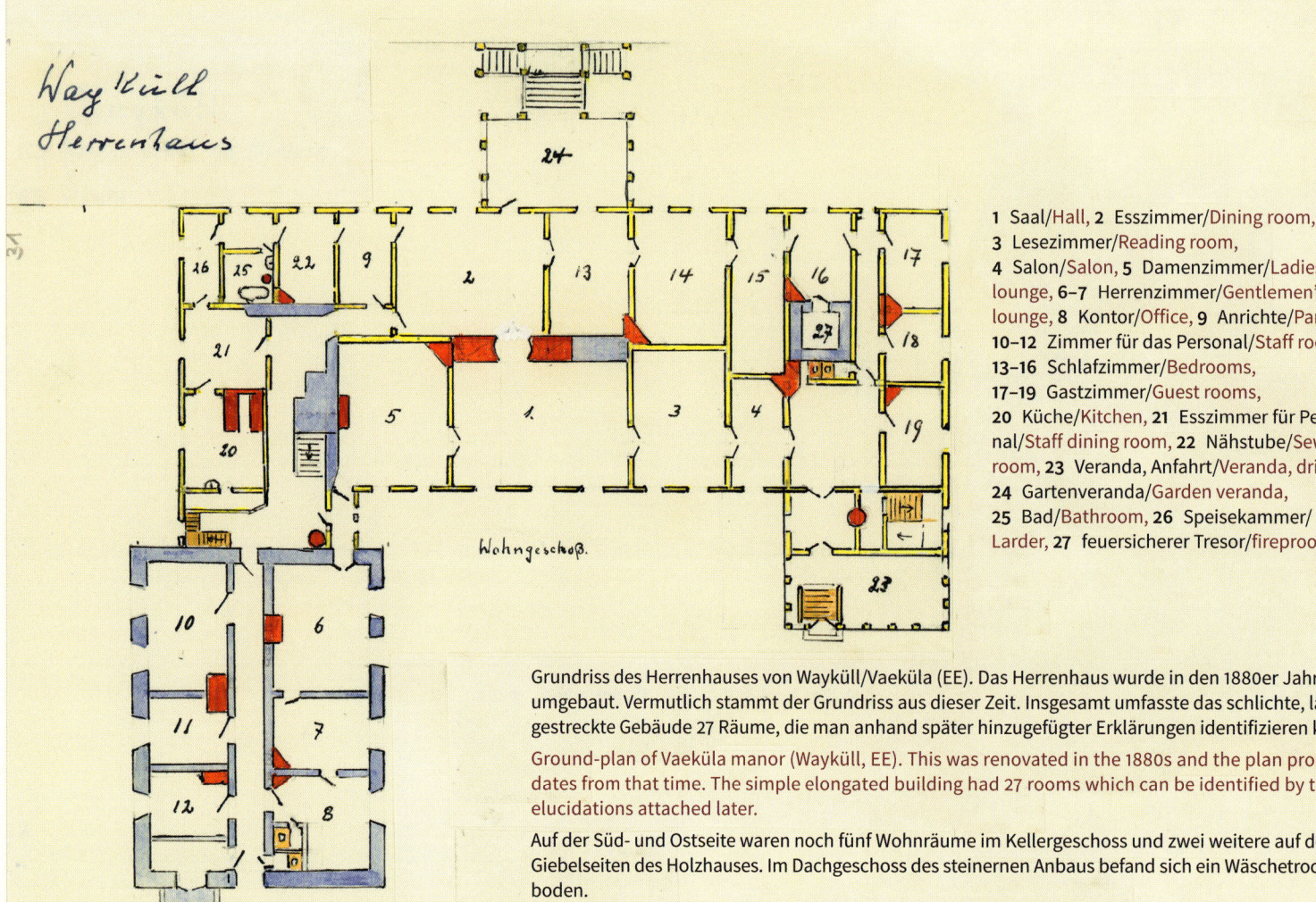

1 Saal/Hall, 2 Esszimmer/Dining room, 3 Lesezimmer/Reading room, 4 Salon/Salon, 5 Damenzimmer/Ladies lounge, 6–7 Herrenzimmer/Gentlemen's lounge, 8 Kontor/Office, 9 Anrichte/Pantry, 10–12 Zimmer für das Personal/Staff rooms, 13–16 Schlafzimmer/Bedrooms, 17–19 Gastzimmer/Guest rooms, 20 Küche/Kitchen, 21 Esszimmer für Personal/Staff dining room, 22 Nähstube/Sewing room, 23 Veranda, Anfahrt/Veranda, drive, 24 Gartenveranda/Garden veranda, 25 Bad/Bathroom, 26 Speisekammer/Larder, 27 feuersicherer Tresor/fireproof safe

Grundriss des Herrenhauses von Wayküll/Vaeküla (EE). Das Herrenhaus wurde in den 1880er Jahren umgebaut. Vermutlich stammt der Grundriss aus dieser Zeit. Insgesamt umfasste das schlichte, langgestreckte Gebäude 27 Räume, die man anhand später hinzugefügter Erklärungen identifizieren kann.

Ground-plan of Vaeküla manor (Wayküll, EE). This was renovated in the 1880s and the plan probably dates from that time. The simple elongated building had 27 rooms which can be identified by the elucidations attached later.

Auf der Süd- und Ostseite waren noch fünf Wohnräume im Kellergeschoss und zwei weitere auf den Giebelseiten des Holzhauses. Im Dachgeschoss des steinernen Anbaus befand sich ein Wäschetrockenboden.

On the south and east side of the house there were five additional living rooms in the cellar, and two more on the gable sides of the wooden construction. In the attic of the stone extension was an area for laundry drying.

Scheune auf dem ehemaligen Gut Kabillen/Kabile (LV, s. a. S. 22). Die mit Arkaden aufwendig gestaltete Fassade des im 18. Jahrhundert errichteten Zweckbaus zeigt die bis ins 19. Jahrhundert verbreitete Tradition, auch rein funktionale Gutsgebäude, die zum Ensemble um das Herrenhaus gehörten, künstlerisch zu gestalten.

Barn on the former Kabile estate (Kabillen, LV, see also p. 22). The facade, amply adorned with arcades, of this 18th century utilitarian building demonstrates a tradition that was widespread until well into the 19th century: even purely functional estate buildings, forming part of the ensemble around a manor house, were artistically embellished.

Natur und Technik
Modernisierung der Gutsanlage

Mit dem Einzug der Technik in der Landwirtschaft im 19. Jahrhundert löste sich die enge räumliche Einheit von Herrenhaus und Wirtschaftsteil des Gutes auf. Die zuvor dem Herrenhaus räumlich und architektonisch untergeordneten Wirtschaftsgebäude wurden gemäß ihrer Funktion zu Gruppen zusammengefasst und zweckmäßig gestaltet. Um das Herrenhaus entstanden ausgedehnte Parkanlagen im englischen Stil, d. h. der natürlichen Landschaft entsprechend bzw. in sie imitierender Gestaltung mit Spazierwegen, sorgfältig angelegten Pflanzengruppen und Kleinarchitekturen, künstlichen Ruinen, Brücken und Gewässern. In den weitläufigen Parks fanden infolge des Bestattungsverbots in Kirchen seit dem ausgehenden 18. Jahrhundert auch Familiengrablegen und Grabdenkmäler Platz. Wie bei den Großbauten folgten sie dem jeweils aktuellen Zeitstil und wurden sowohl von bekannten Zeitgenossen wie Johann Georg Berlitz (1753–1837) als auch von einheimischen Baumeistern errichtet, deren Namen nicht überliefert sind.

Mit den nächsten Ortschaften und Städten waren die Güter bis zur Mitte des 19. Jahrhunderts meistens über Landstraßen verbunden. Seit dem späten 19. Jahrhundert kümmerten sich Landbesitzer verstärkt um die Modernisierung der Verkehrsinfrastruktur in den Ostseeprovinzen, vor allem um den Ausbau des wirtschaftlich notwendigen Eisenbahnnetzes. Die Hauptstrecken des Zugverkehrs in Estland und Lettland wurden in dieser Zeit angelegt.

Nature and Technology
Modernisation of Estate Infrastructure

The close spatial unity of manor house and the estate's working sector disappeared with the arrival of technology in 19th century agriculture. Farm buildings, which had previously been subordinated spatially and architecturally to the manor house, were now grouped according to function and use. Extended park areas in the English style were established around the manor house – either as natural landscapes or imitations of such with a structure of walkways, careful groupings of plants, buildings and artificial ruins, bridges, and stretches of water. There were also family graves and funeral monuments in these expansive parks as a result of the ban on burial in churches from the end of the 18th century. Like the larger buildings these followed contemporary styles and were created by such well-known architects as Johann Georg Berlitz (1753–1837) and local builders whose names have been lost.

Manor houses were linked by country roads with the nearest villages and towns until the mid-19th century. From later that century the land-owning nobility was increasingly involved in modernisation of transportation infrastructure in the Baltic provinces and primarily with extension of the economically necessary railway network. The main rail links in Estonia and Latvia were established during that period.

S. 56: Parkanlage auf dem Gut Burtneck/Burtnieki (LV) mit Pavillon. Der große Park mit gleichmäßig angelegten Beeten, Wegen und ornamental arrangierter Bepflanzung entstand in der zweiten Hälfte des 19. Jahrhunderts. Erhalten hat sich nur der monumental anmutende Pavillon aus Holz. Diese neobarocke Anlage stand im deutlichen Gegensatz zum einstigen Herrenhaus, das ein schlichter, längsrechteckiger und fast dekorloser Bau war. Foto vor 1935

p. 56: Park with pavilion on the Burtnieki (Burtneck, LV) estate. This extensive park with regular flower-beds, winding paths, and ornamental plant arrangements was created in the second half of the 19th century, but all that remains today is the monumental wooden pavilion. This neo-baroque park contrasted strongly with the former residence which was a simple, almost undecorated, rectangular building. Photo before 1935

Grabdenkmal der Fürstin Charlotte von Lieven (1743–1828) im Schlosspark von Mesothen/Mežotne (LV, s. a. S. 30 f., 42, 45, 68). Die geadelte Erzieherin der Kinder der Zarin war die Erbauerin und Besitzerin des Herrenhauses Mesothen/Mežotne. Foto ca. 1938

Monument to Princess Charlotte von Lieven (1743–1828) in the Mežotne park (Mesothen, LV, see also pp. 30 f., 42, 45, 68). The ennobled governess of the Tsarina's children commissioned and owned this manor house. Photo ca. 1938

Der Alexander-Pavillon im Schlosspark Marienburg/Alūksne (LV). Schon seit dem Mittelalter galt Marienburg als eine wichtige Grenzstadt zu Russland. Die enge Beziehung des deutschbaltischen Adels zum Zarenhof zeigt sich beispielhaft in dem nach dem russischen Zaren Alexander I. benannten Pavillon im Park des Gutshofs. Foto vor 1935

The Alexander Pavilion in the Alūksne park (Marienburg, LV). From the Middle Ages Alūksne had been an important town on the border with Russia. The German-Baltic gentry's close relationship with the Tsar's court is exemplified in this pavilion named after Alexander I. Photo before 1935

Postkarte mit der Darstellung der Brauerei Kokenhof/Kokmuiža (LV). In der Bierbrauerei von Kokenhof wurde seit der Mitte des 19. Jahrhunderts industriell produziert. Die Braumeister kamen aus München. Heute stellt eine Brauerei in Wolmarshof/Valmiermuiža (LV) wieder Bier nach Rezepten von Kokenhof her. Rechts im Bild ist das Herrenhaus mit Gutshof und Parkanlage zu sehen.

A postcard depicting the Kokmuiža brewery (Kokenhof, LV). Brewing beer took place on an industrial scale from the mid-19th century. The master brewers came from Munich. Today a brewery in Valmiermuiža (Wolmarshof, LV) is once again using Kokenhof recipes. The manor house is on the right of the picture with its courtyard and the park-like landscape.

Eisenbahnbaustelle in Estland zwischen Kegel/Keila und Hapsal/Haapsalu. Diese 1905 fertiggestellte Strecke war ein Teil der Verbindung zwischen Reval/Tallinn und dem Ende des 19. Jahrhunderts auch bei der russischen Zarenfamilie sehr beliebten Kurort Hapsal/Haapsalu. Foto 1900

Establishing the Estonian railway between Keila (Kegel) and Haapsalu (Hapsal). This stretch, completed in 1905, was part of the link between Tallinn (Reval) and the spa town of Haapsalu (Hapsal), much favoured by the Russian Tsar's family at the end of the 19th century. Photo 1900

Von Rang und Stand
Grundbesitz und Selbstverständnis

Im Laufe der Zeit wechselten aus verschiedenen Gründen die Besitzer eines Herrenhauses. Den Gutsbesitz konnte man vom Landesherrn als Lehen erhalten, ihn erben, durch Heirat in seinen Besitz kommen oder ihn kaufen bzw. pachten. Für Leistungen im Staatsdienst oder aufgrund eines Amtes gelangten zahlreiche Güter als Geschenk des Landesherrn in den Besitz von Begünstigten. Konsolidierung und Vergrößerung des Grundbesitzes war eine wichtige Aufgabe der Gutsherrschaft. Doch konnte es auch zum Verlust von Ländereien kommen. Manchmal erzwang wirtschaftlicher Bankrott oder Überschuldung den Verkauf und damit den Besitzerwechsel eines Gutes.

Die Inhaber von Pastoraten genossen dieselben Vorrechte wie die anderer Güter. Jedoch war ihr Besitzrecht auf die Dienstzeit als Pastor beschränkt. Ein Pastor wurde von Kirchenvorstehern gewählt oder von einem oder mehreren Patronen – rekrutiert aus dem grundbesitzenden Adel – bestimmt und konnte bei Streitigkeiten auch vorzeitig abgesetzt werden.

Ranking and Status
Landed Property and Self-Image

Over the course of time there were changes – for various reasons – in ownership of manor houses. Estates could be granted in fief, inherited, acquired through marriage, bought, or leased. Ownership of many manor houses was transferred as a sovereign's gift in recognition of services to the state or as an attribute of public office. Consolidation and enlargement of an estate was an important task for landowners. But landholdings could also be lost. Sometimes economic bankruptcy or indebtedness made necessary sale of an estate and thus a change of ownership.

Owners of parish land enjoyed similar rights, but ownership was limited to the clergyman's time in office there. A parish priest was chosen by the chairman of the parish council or by one or several patrons (recruited from the land-owning gentry) and in case of dispute could be prematurely dismissed.

◀ Herrenhaus Appricken/Apriķi (LV) von der Gartenseite mit dem Allianzwappen der Familie von Osten-Sacken und von Korff im Giebelfeld. Das Haus wurde anlässlich der Heirat des Erbauers Christoph Friedrich von Osten-Sacken (1697–1759) in der Mitte des 18. Jahrhunderts errichtet.

◀ Apriķi manor house (Appricken, LV) seen from the garden with a coat of arms uniting the Osten-Sacken and von Korff families on the gable. The house was built in the mid-18th century in celebration of the marriage of Christoph Friedrich von Osten-Sacken (1697–1759).

◀ Herrenhaus Seßwegen/Cesvaine (LV). Das Gebäude auf u-förmigem Grundriss entstand von 1890 bis 1897 nach Entwürfen der Architekten Hans Grisebach (1848–1904) und August Georg Dinklage (1849–1920) unter Verwendung von Stilelementen der Romanik, Gotik und Renaissance.

◀ Cesvaine manor (Seßwegen, LV). This was constructed on a U-shaped ground-plan between 1890 and 1897. The designs by architects Hans Grisebach (1848–1904) and August Georg Dinklage (1849–1920) incorporated Romanesque, Gothic, and Renaissance stylistic elements.

Herrenhaus Seßwegen/Cesvaine (LV). Die Giebelbekrönung in Form eines Wolfs spielt auf das Wappentier der Familie von Wulff an, der Erbauer und Besitzer des neogotischen Herrenhauses.

Cesvaine manor house (Seßwegen, LV). The gable is crowned with the figure of a wolf, alluding to the coat of arms of the von Wulff family which built and owned this neo-gothic dwelling.

Carl Timoleon von Neff: Ansicht von Schloss Löwenhof/Kuigatsi (EE), Öl auf Papier, 2. Hälfte des 19. Jahrhunderts, 14 x 19,6 cm ohne Rahmen

Von Neff, bekannt als Historien-, Porträt- und Genremaler, gibt in diesem kleinformatigen Gemälde Mitglieder der Besitzerfamilie Löwenstern im Garten vor dem Herrenhaus wieder. Das spätbarocke Haus wurde in den 1770/80er Jahren aus Holz auf einem steinernen Sockel errichtet. Von der Familie stammt der deutsche Name »Löwenhof« für das Gut (seit 1803), das ursprünglich »Kuikatz« hieß.

Carl Timoleon von Neff: Kuigatsi manor house (Löwenhof, EE), oil on paper, 2. half of the 19th century, 14 x 19,6 cm without frame

In this small painting, von Neff, known for his historical scenes, portraits, and depictions of everyday life, presents members of the Löwenstern family in the garden in front of the manor they owned. The late-baroque building was constructed of wood on a stone foundation in the 1770s and 1780s. The German name for the estate, »Löwenhof« (from 1803), derived from this surname. Originally it was called »Kuikatz«.

G. Parrini: Porträt von Carl Timoleon von Neff (1804–1876/77). Von Neff war Hofmaler und Konservator am kaiserlich russischen Hof sowie Bauherr und Besitzer des Herrenhauses Münkenhof/Muuga möis (EE). Teile seiner großen Kunstsammlung befinden sich heute im Estnischen Kunstmuseum in Reval/Eesti Kunstimuuseum (Kumu) Tallinn.

G. Parrini: Portrait of Carl Timoleon von Neff (1804–1876/77). Von Neff was a court painter and conservationist for the Russian Tsar. He also commissioned the Muuga manor house (Münkenhof, EE) as his own residence. Today works from his large art collection are in the Estonian art museum/Eesti Kunstimuuseum (Kumu) at Tallinn (Reval).

S. 6: Herrenhaus Münkenhof/Muuga (EE). Die ersten Nachrichten über das Gut stammen aus dem 16. Jahrhundert. 1860 erwarb es Timoleon von Neff und ließ das Herrenhaus zwischen 1866 und 1872 errichten. Es ist ein charakteristisches Beispiel für die Neorenaissance.

p. 6: Muuga manor (Münkenhof, EE). The first reference to this estate dates from the 16th century. In 1860 is was bought by Timoleon von Neff. He commissioned construction (between 1866 and 1872) of the manor house in a neo-renaissance style.

Bauern und Bedienstete
Arbeit auf dem Gutshof

In den Ostseeprovinzen waren die vom Gutshof abhängigen, untertänigen Bauern bis zur Aufhebung der Leibeigenschaft 1816/1819 zu Frondiensten auf den Gutsländereien und Abgaben verpflichtet. Ihre Arbeitsleistung wurde je nach Anzahl des Gesindes nach Tagen bemessen und in sogenannten Wackenbüchern für Bauern wie Gutsherren verbindlich verzeichnet. Auch nach Erlangung der persönlichen Freiheit und der Möglichkeit zum Landerwerb seit der Mitte des 19. Jahrhunderts blieben Bauern mit dem Gutsherrn bis zur Ablösung der Geldleistungen für den Landkauf verbunden. Hofleute wie das Hauspersonal (Zimmer- und Küchenmädchen etc.), Krüger und Handwerker waren unmittelbare Bedienstete der Familie des Gutsherrn. Die (Neben-)Güter, die von den Adelsfamilien nicht bewohnt wurden, unterstanden einem bezahlten Amtmann, einem Gutsverwalter.

Als keinem Gut fron- und abgabepflichtig galt der Stand der Freibauern, zu denen deutsche Kleinlandwirte und Nachkommen estnischer und lettischer Stammesältester gehörten, die seit alters her durch die Landesherren privilegiert waren. Sie genossen persönliche und steuerliche Freiheit, leisteten im Gegenzug Kriegs- oder Verwaltungsdienste.

◀ Erntearbeit mit Maschinen in Mesothen/Mežotne (LV, s. a. S. 30 f., 42, 45, 58). Die Mehrzahl der Feldarbeiten wurde von Gutsbediensteten per Hand erledigt. Beim Korndreschen kamen auf den großen Gütern seit der zweiten Hälfte des 19. Jahrhunderts Dampfdreschmaschinen aus englischer und amerikanischer Produktion zum Einsatz. Foto vor 1935

Peasants and Servants
Work on the Estate

In the Baltic governorates peasants were dependent on and subservient to landed estates until abolition of serfdom in 1816/19. They were obliged to work for and pay levies to lords of the manor. Their work contribution depended on the number of farmhands, the number of days worked and binding contributions in kind as recorded in work-books *(Wackenbücher)*. Even after the mid-19th century when peasants had gained personal freedom and the possibility of buying land, they still remained bound to landowners until the abolition of special charges for such purchases. Domestic staff (house- and kitchen-maids, etc.) as well as innkeepers and skilled workers were directly employed by the landowner's family. Smaller properties, which were not directly inhabited by noble families, were run by a paid estate manager.

Free peasants' status relieved them of the obligation to supply labour or levies. They included German smallholders and the offspring of Estonian and Latvian tribal elders whom the sovereigns had privileged from time immemorial. They enjoyed personal freedom and exemption from taxes, and in return served in wars or local administration.

◀ Harvesting with machines at Mežotne (Mesothen, LV, see also pp. 30 f., 42, 45, 58). Most field-work was done by hand by estate employees. English and American steam threshing machines were used on large estates from the second half of the 19th century. Photo before 1935

69

Bauernhof in Kurland bei Alt-Autz/Vecauce (LV). Die meisten Bauernhöfe im Baltikum hatten bis zur Mitte des 19. Jahrhunderts bescheidene Ausmaße und waren überwiegend aus Holz gebaut. Mit der Möglichkeit des Landerwerbs im Zuge der Bauernbefreiung konnten die Höfe vergrößert und Steinbauten errichtet werden. Foto vor 1920

Farmhouse in Courland near Vecauce (Alt-Autz, LV). Until the mid-19th century most farmhouses in the Baltic area were modest in size and largely constructed of wood. When the granting of freedom to peasants brought the possibility of buying land, farms could become larger and stone buildings erected. Photo before 1920

Aufgeschlagenes Wackenbuch des Gutes Palms/Palmse (EE, s. a. S. 24 ff., 50 f.), 1733.

Open work-book *(Wackenbuch)* from the Palmse estate (Palms, EE, see also pp. 24 ff., 50 f.), 1733.

Selbstsicht und Fremdsicht
Gutsbewohner im Bild

Im Unterschied zu den aus der vermögenden Oberschicht stammenden Gutsbesitzern, deren Porträts und Ahnengalerien ganze Wände in den baltischen Herrenhäusern füllten, sind gemalte oder fotografische Bildnisse ihrer Bediensteten und Bauern sehr viel seltener. Das unterstreicht die Bedeutung der gezeichneten Porträts, die der livländische Pastor Anton Georg Bosse (1792–1860) in den Jahren 1857 bis 1860 von Menschen aus seiner Gemeinde Alt-Wohlfahrt/ Ēvele (LV) und der nächsten Umgebung anfertigte. Unter dem Einfluss der im historischen Livland starken protestantischen Herrnhuter Bewegung hat der Autor jedes Bildnis mit Namen versehen und mit berufsspezifischen Merkmalen individuell charakterisiert. Im Gegensatz zu diesen leicht idealisierten Bildnissen von Bosse zeichnete nur wenige Jahre zuvor Sophie von Hahn (1804–1863) ein anderes Bild von den Bauern in den russischen Ostseeprovinzen. Die Vernachlässigung durch die baltischen Gutsherren anklagend, berichtete sie, die Bauern kämmten sich nur sonntags und wechselten die Kleidung wochentags nicht.

Seen by Oneself and by Others
Depictions of Estate-Dwellers

Portraits and other ancestral mementos of property-owners from the affluent upper class filled entire walls in Baltic manor houses, but there are far fewer painted or photographic depictions of their servants and peasants. That enhances the significance of drawings, produced between 1857 and 1860 by Anton Georg Bosse (1792–1860), a Livonian pastor, of people from his Ēvele parish (Alt-Wohlfahrt, LV) and its immediate surroundings. Influenced by the Moravian Church (Herrnhuter), highly influential in Old-Livonia, Bosse added to each depiction an individual name and vocationally specific information. These slightly idealized images contrast with the different picture of peasants in the Russian Baltic provinces presented by Sophie von Hahn (1804–1863) a few years earlier. Lamenting their neglect by Baltic landowners, she reports that peasants only combed their hair on Sundays and did not change their clothes during the week.

◀ Drei Frauen und ein Mädchen auf einem Holzstapel in Lappier/ Ozolmuiža (LV, s. a. S. 8, 90). Die abgebildeten, namentlich nicht bekannten Personen gehörten wohl zum Gutshof. Welche Funktion und Stellung sie dort einnahmen, ist unbekannt. Foto vor 1935

◀ Three women and a girl on a heap of logs in Ozolmuiža (Lappier, LV, see also pp. 8, 90). The unnamed persons depicted were probably employed in the farmhouse. Their function and position are unknown. Photo before 1935

Herrenhaus Semershof/Ziemeri (LV). Saal im Herrenhaus mit Porträts der Familie von Wolff, in deren Besitz sich das Gut seit 1810 befand. Foto vor 1935

Manor house Ziemeri (Semershof, LV). Hall with portraits of the von Wolff family, owners of the estate since 1810. Photo before 1935

Herrenhaus Asuppen/Aizupe (LV, s. a. S. 43, 46). Das Arbeitszimmer ist im Stil des für die erste Hälfte des 19. Jahrhunderts charakteristischen Biedermeiers eingerichtet, mit Porträts über der Sitzecke und zu beiden Seiten des Kamins. Foto 1924

Aizupe manor house (Asuppen, LV, see also pp. 43, 46). The study is furnished in the Biedermeier style characteristic of the first half of the 19th century with portraits above the seating area and on both sides of the chimney. Photo 1924

Anton Georg Bosse: Der Wirt und Weber Lībis Liepiņš, 1857
Anton Georg Bosse: Innkeeper and weaver Lībis Liepiņš, 1857

Anton Georg Bosse: Porträt Katrīne Briede, 1858. Das Buch in der Hand der Wirtin weist auf ihr Lesevermögen hin. Es ist aber auch ein Zeichen, dass sie eine gute Christin ist. Gerade die dem Pietismus nahestehenden Pfarrer legten großen Wert darauf, dass die Gläubigen die Bibel lasen. Frauen als Mütter und Erzieherinnen kam dabei eine bedeutende Rolle zu. In der Mitte des 19. Jahrhunderts konnte ein großer Teil der einfachen Bevölkerung lesen und schreiben.

Anton Georg Bosse's portrait of Katrīne Briede, 1858. The book held by the innkeeper's wife indicates a capacity to read. Pietistic clergymen placed great value on believers being able to read the Bible. There women as mothers and teachers played an important part. By the mid-19th century a large part of the workaday population could read and write.

Geschichte der Gutshöfe nach 1900

Estates viewed historically since 1900

Entbrannter Zorn
Gutshöfe in Revolution und Krieg

Im Zuge der Russischen Revolution von 1905, bei der es auch in den Ostseeprovinzen zu gewaltsamen Ausschreitungen kam, wurden etwa 200 Herrenhäuser geplündert und niedergebrannt. Der Zorn der aufständischen Esten und Letten richtete sich gegen Gutsbesitzer, Staatsbeamte und Pfarrer, die willkürlich gefangen und ermordet wurden.

Nach der Niederschlagung der Revolte ließen viele Gutsbesitzer, die im Land geblieben waren, ihre Häuser wiederaufbauen. Dabei sollte das Herrenhaus möglichst nah am Original restauriert werden. Es war ein Versuch, die Blütezeit der Gutsherrschaft im 18. und 19. Jahrhundert neu zu beleben. Eine detailtreue Rekonstruktion des klassizistischen Schlosses Katzdangen/Kazdanga (LV) gelang dem deutschen Architekten Paul Schulze-Naumburg (1869–1949) im Auftrag von Carl Baron Manteuffel-Szoege (1872–1948). Es ist ein frühes Beispiel einer sorgfältigen und wissenschaftlich fundierten Wiederherstellung im Sinne moderner Denkmalpflege. Auf Wunsch der Auftraggeber kleideten die Architekten die Häuser aber auch in bestimmte historisierende Stile, um die Illusion eines altehrwürdigen, über Generationen gewachsenen Hauses zu schaffen.

Nur wenige Jahre später waren die Gutshöfe und vor allem die Herrenhäuser durch den Ersten Weltkrieg und die Russische Revolution von 1917 neuen Zerstörungen ausgesetzt. Das Militär nutze fast alle Herrenhäuser für kriegsbezogene Zwecke. Einige, wie das herausragende klassizistische Herrenhaus in Elley/Eleja (LV, s. a. S. 31, 35), wurden infolge von Kampfhandlungen stark beschädigt oder zerstört.

Eruption of Rage
Manor Houses during Revolution and War

During the 1905 revolution in Russia there were also violent clashes in the Baltic governorates, and around 200 manor houses were plundered and burned down. The rage of rebellious Estonians and Latvians was directed against the nobility, local administrators, and clergymen who were arbitrarily captured and murdered.

After the uprisings had been suppressed many of the landowners who remained in the country had their properties rebuilt. Their intention was that such buildings should be restored as closely as possible to the original. That was an attempt at restoring their time of flourishing in the 18th and 19th centuries. Paul Schulze-Naumburg (1869–1949), a German architect, was commissioned by Carl Baron Manteuffel-Szoege (1872–1948) to undertake faithful reconstruction of the neoclassical residence at Kazdanga (Katzdangen, LV). This is an early example of careful and scholarly preservation of historical monuments in accordance with modern principles. Architects also followed their clients' wishes in utilising specific historic styles so as to create the illusion of a venerable house which had grown across generations.

Just a few years later these estates and particularly its manor houses were once again exposed to renewed destruction during the First World War and the Russian Revolution of 1917. The military used almost all manor houses for war-related purposes. Some, such as the outstanding neoclassical residence at Eleja (Elley, LV, see also pp. 31, 35), were greatly damaged or destroyed in armed clashes.

S. 80: Herrenhaus Katzdangen/Kazdanga (LV), um 1800 von Johann Georg Berlitz (1753–1837) im Auftrag der Familie Manteuffel-Szoege errichtet und nach 1905 von Paul Schulze-Naumburg detailgetreu wiederhergestellt.

p. 80: Kazdanga manor house (Katzdangen, LV), constructed around 1800 by Johann Georg Berlitz (1753–1837) for the Manteuffel-Szoege family, and faithfully restored after 1905 by Paul Schulze-Naumburg.

Friedrich Baron Wolff-Lettien (1883–1943) vor einem Gebäude in Alt-Karmel/Asuküla (EE). Ihm ist eine Vielzahl wertvoller historischer Aufnahmen baltischer Guts- und Herrenhäuser aus dem frühen 20. Jahrhundert zu verdanken. Etwa 4 000 Negative seiner ursprünglich vermutlich bedeutend größeren, in den 1920/30er Jahren durchgeführten Dokumentation befinden sich im Bestand des Bildarchivs des Herder-Instituts. Foto vor 1935

Friedrich Baron Wolff-Lettien (1883–1943) in front of a building in Asuküla (Alt-Karmel, EE). He took many historically valuable photographs of Baltic houses dating from the early 20th century. Around 4 000 negatives from this probably originally much larger collection are now in the Herder Institute's archive. Photo before 1935

Stomersee — Walkscher Kreis.

Besitzer: Hofmeister Boris Baron Wolff und Paul Baron Wolff.

Eingeäschert im Winter 1905.

Schloss Stomersee/Stāmeriena (LV, s. a. S. 38) war im Besitz von Hofmeister Boris Baron Wolff und Paul Baron Wolff. Es brannte im Zuge der Revolution im Winter 1905 aus, wurde jedoch 1908 wiederaufgebaut.

This Stāmeriena (Stomersee, LV, see also p. 38) country residence was owned by Boris Baron Wolff, Lord High Steward, and Paul Baron Wolff. It was burned down in winter 1905 during the Revolution, but rebuilt in 1908.

Schloss Dondangen/Dundaga (LV, s. a. S. 14), Ostseite, während des Wiederaufbaus 1911. Die Burg Dondangen, vom Deutschen Orden errichtet und 1318 erstmals urkundlich erwähnt, wurde ab dem 17. Jahrhundert den Erfordernissen als Gutshaus gemäß umgebaut. Während der Revolution 1905 brannte das Gebäude nieder. Nach den Entwürfen des Braunschweiger Architekten Hermann Pfeiffer erfolgte 1909 ein Wiederaufbau. Seit 1926 wurde das Schloss als Schule sowie als Verwaltungsgebäude genutzt.

Dundaga manor (Dondangen, LV, see also p. 14), seen from the East, during reconstruction in 1911. Dondangen was built as a fortress by the Livonian Order and first mentioned in documents in 1318. This was reconverted in the 17th century to meet the requirements of a large country house. It was burned down in 1905 and rebuilt in 1909 following plans by Brunswick architect Hermann Pfeiffer. Since 1926 it has been utilised as both a school and an administrative centre.

Gutshaus Groß-Roop/Lielstraupe (LV), seit dem Mittelalter im Besitz der Familie von Rosen. Das malerische Gutsensemble wurde 1905 in Brand gesteckt und unmittelbar danach bis 1910 von Wilhelm Bockslaff (1858–1945) rekonstruiert. Von 1963 bis 2017 beherbergte das Herrenhaus eine Heilanstalt für Suchtkranke. Die Zukunft der stark renovierungsbedürftigen Anlage ist aktuell ungeklärt.

Lielstraupe manor house (Gross-Roop, LV), owned by the von Rosen family since the Middle Ages. This picturesque ensemble of buildings was set on fire in 1905 and immediately rebuilt in the five years that followed by Wilhelm Bockslaff (1858–1945). From 1963 to 2017 the manor housed a sanatorium for people with addiction problems. The building is now in urgent need of repair and its future is uncertain.

Baltische Tragödie
Das Ende der Gutsherrschaft

Nach dem Untergang des russischen Zarenreichs entstanden am Ende des Ersten Weltkrieges 1918 die Nationalstaaten Estland und Lettland. Die dadurch erfolgte Zweiteilung des historischen Livland nach Sprachgrenzen brach radikal mit der bisherigen territorialen Ordnung und der kulturellen Tradition der Region. Die Agrarreform von 1919/20, durch die die Gutsbesitzer bis auf fünfzig Hektar Restgut enteignet wurden, versetzte der alten Elite einen weiteren Schlag. Die wirtschaftliche (und politische) Vormachtstellung des deutschbaltischen Adels war damit beendet. Der Unterhalt der großen Herrenhäuser und Anwesen wurde unmöglich. Einige Restgüter konnten unter Anstrengungen noch bis 1939 bewirtschaftet werden, doch viele Gutshäuser wurden bereits in den 1920er Jahren verlassen. Zahlreiche Güter übernahm der Staat und richtete in den Herrenhäusern und anderen Gebäuden Schulen, Heime und Heilanstalten ein, die oft bis heute die Häuser bewirtschaften. Um die Erinnerung an die frühere Gutsherrschaft gründlich auszulöschen, wurden alle Orts- und Straßennamen im jungen Staat Lettland, die den Begriff »Gut« beinhalteten, getilgt oder geändert. Die Umsiedlung der Deutschbalten im Zuge des Hitler-Stalin-Paktes ab Herbst 1939 bedeutete das Ende dieser Minderheit in Estland und Lettland.

◂ Das Herrenhaus Ratshof/Raadi (EE, s. a. S. 34, 43, 45) ist ein Beispiel für eine Neunutzung mit besonders hoher Symbolkraft. In dem zum Nationalmuseum umgewandelten Herrenhaus stellte man nun estnisches Kunsthandwerk statt europäische Kunstwerke aus. In elf Güterwaggons konnte die Familie Liphart einen Großteil ihrer Kunstschätze nach Deutschland ausführen. Ein Drittel ihrer Sammlung schenkte sie dem jungen estnischen Staat.

Baltic Tragedy
The End of Lords of the Manor

After the fall of the Russian Tsarist Empire the nation-states of Estonia and Latvia came into existence at the end of the First World War in 1918. The resultant division of Old Livonia in accordance with linguistic borders radically breached the region's previous territorial structure and cultural tradition. Agricultural reform in 1919/20, whereby landowners were dispossessed of all their land except for fifty hectares, was a further blow to the old elite. The economic (and political) dominance of the German Baltic nobility was thus brought to an end. Maintenance of the great manor houses and their estates became impossible. Some of the land that remained could still be farmed, with difficulty, until 1939, but many of the houses were abandoned as early as the 1920s. The state took over many estates and established schools, welfare facilities, and sanatoriums which have often made use of these buildings up to the present day. In the new state of Latvia the names of places and streets that included the word *Gut* (estate) were eradicated or changed as to wipe out memories of former manorial dominance. Resettlement of Baltic Germans from 1939 following the German-Soviet Non-Aggression Pact meant the end of this minority in Estonia and Latvia.

◂ Raadi manor (Ratshof, EE, see also pp. 34, 43, 45) is a particularly symbolic example of a former country residence being taken over by new owners. Raadi has now been transformed into the Estonian National Museum with local (Estonian) arts and crafts on show rather than European works of art. The Liphart family managed to export a considerable part of their artistic treasures to Germany in eleven goods wagons. The family donated a third of its collection to the new state of Estonia.

Grundriss des früheren Herrenhauses Riddeldorf/Rideļi (LV) mit Markierung des als Restgut verbliebenen und für die ehemaligen Gutsherren nutzbaren Teils des Hauses. Der Plan aus dem Nachlass der Familie der Grafen Lambsdorff befindet sich in der Dokumentesammlung des Herder-Instituts, die zahlreiche herausragende Quellen zur baltischen Gutskultur bewahrt.

Ground-plan of the Rideļi manor house (Riddeldorf, LV), marking what remained for use by the former owners. This plan from the archives of the von Lambsdorff family is now in the Herder Institute's documents collection, which safeguards many outstanding sources relating to Baltic estates.

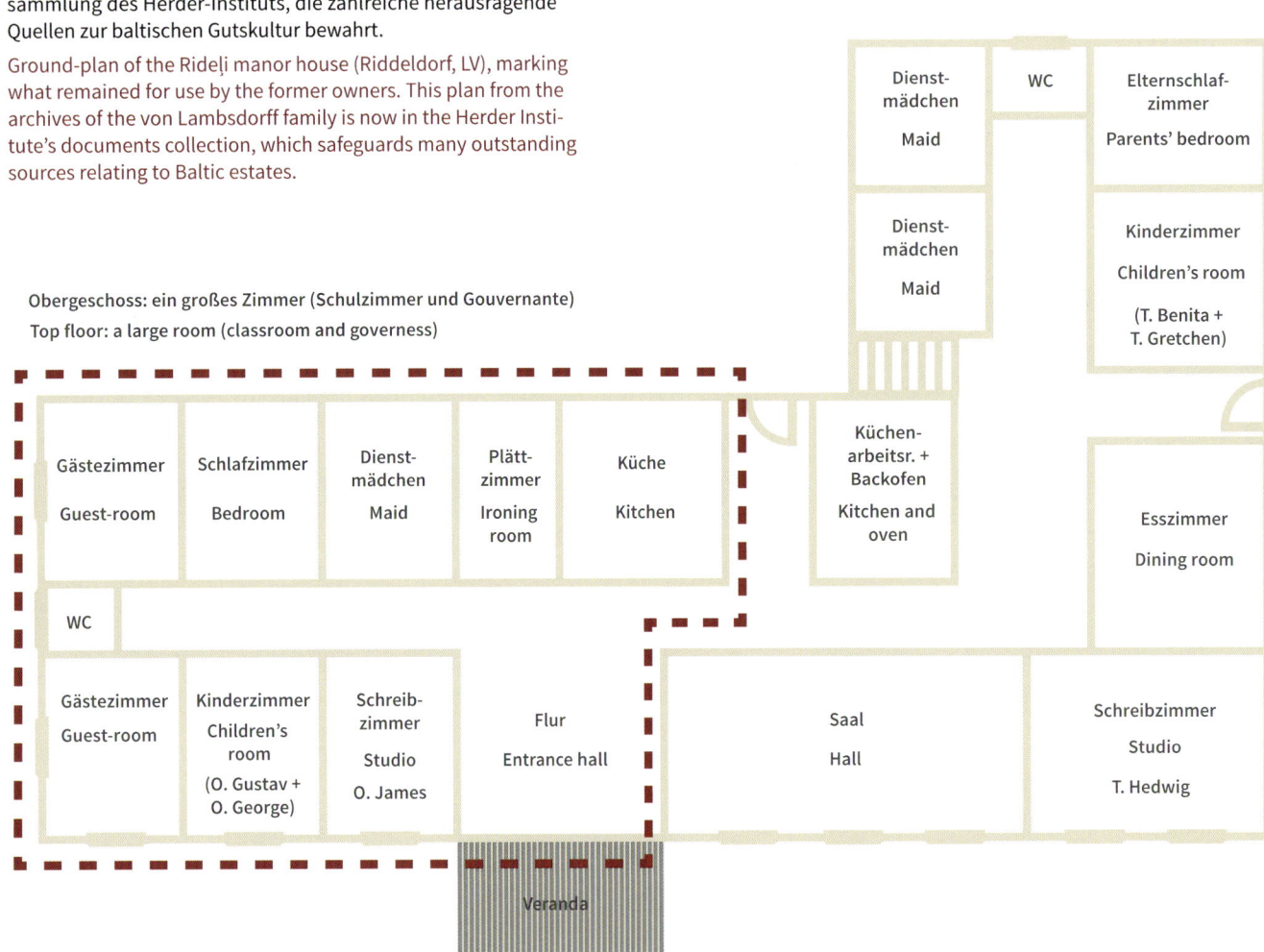

Ansicht des Gutshauses Riddeldorf/Rideļi (LV). Das schlichte Herrenhaus war seit der Mitte des 19. Jahrhunderts bis zur Enteignung im Besitz der Familie der Grafen Lambsdorff. Foto vor 1935

View of Rideļi manor (Riddeldorf, LV). From the mid-19th century this simple building belonged to the von Lambsdorff family until expropriation. Photo before 1935

Herrenhaus Lappier/Ozolmuiža (LV, s. a. S. 8, 72 f.). Der sogenannte Marmorsaal im Herrensitz der Grafen Mellin diente, wie weitere Zimmer auch, nach der Enteignung als Lagerraum. Zu der Zeit, als das Foto entstand (vor 1928), bewohnte die gräfliche Familie, der keine Mittel mehr für die Instandhaltung des Hauses zur Verfügung standen, nur einige wenige Räume.

Ozolmuiža manor (Lappier, LV, see also pp. 8, 72 f.). After expropriation what was known as the marble hall in the manor of the Counts Mellin, and also other rooms, were used for storage. When the photo was taken (before 1928) the landed gentry family no longer had the means to maintain the manor and lived in just a few rooms of their house.

»Gartengrundstücks›besitzer‹ auf dem Platz des Herrenhauses Techelfer/Tähtvere (EE)«. Der aus Estland stammende Bildberichterstatter Karl Hintzer (1895–1967) hat Menschen bei der Feldarbeit auf Grundstücken im Bereich des ehemaligen Guts Techelfer dokumentiert. Die vom Fotografen gewählte Bildunterschrift verweist auf die Vergabe der Grundstücke ehemaliger Gutshöfe nach deren Enteignung 1919 an neue Pächter. Foto vor 1944/45

»Garden-plot ›owners‹ at Tähtvere manor (Techelfer, EE)«. Karl Hintzer (1895–1967), a photojournalist from Estonia, documented work in the fields of the former Tähtvere estate. The photographer's caption refers to the distribution of former manor land to new tenants after the expropriation of 1919. Photo before 1944/45

Ungeliebtes Erbe
Herrenhäuser zur Sowjetzeit

Nach der erzwungenen Eingliederung Estlands und Lettlands in die kommunistisch regierte Sowjetunion 1940 verstärkte sich die feindliche und ablehnende Einstellung gegenüber dem historischen Erbe der ehemaligen Oberschicht, die jetzt nicht nur als fremd angesehen wurde, sondern auch als Klassenfeind galt. Gezielt zerstört wurden die Herrenhäuser nicht, doch viele durch Vernachlässigung dem Verfall preisgegeben. Als Ausdruck der veränderten Machtverhältnisse richtete sich in manchen Herrenhäusern die lokale Kolchosverwaltung ein. Die bauliche Anpassung an die neue Funktion der weitergenutzten Herrenhäuser geschah nicht selten rücksichtslos nach rein funktionalen Gesichtspunkten. Entstellungen und Beschädigungen der ursprünglichen Gestaltung und Ausstattung nahm man dabei in Kauf. So wurden beispielsweise Anbauten aus Silikat-Ziegeln errichtet, die Raumanordnung durch Entfernen von Wänden verändert oder größere Räume zu Sporthallen umfunktioniert. Andere Herrenhäuser wurden zu Mietshäusern mit mehreren Wohnungen umgebaut.

Den ehemaligen Besitzern blieben von ihren Herrenhäusern nicht viel mehr als Erinnerungen, ein paar Einrichtungsgegenstände oder Fotos. Durch Nachbauten ganzer Interieurs versuchten manche von ihnen das Ambiente ihres einstigen Herrenhauses und das damit verbundene Lebensgefühl in ihrem neuen Wohnsitz zu bewahren.

◂ Herrenhaus Kortenhof/Beļava (LV). Das unzerstört gebliebene Herrenhaus dient seit 1926 als Grundschule. Im Inneren haben sich einige dekorative Elemente der ursprünglichen barocken Ausstattung wie Deckenstuck, Wandpaneele, eingebaute Schränke und Türschmuck erhalten.

Unloved Inheritance
Manor Houses Under Soviet Rule

After enforced integration of Estonia and Latvia into the communist-ruled Soviet Union in 1940, there was intensification of hostile and dismissive attitudes towards the historic legacy of the former upper class, now seen as both foreigners and a class-enemies. Manor houses were not deliberately destroyed but many were allowed to go to rack and ruin through neglect. Changed power relationships were demonstrated by the establishment of administrative offices for local collective farms (kolkhozes) in some manor houses. Not infrequently conversion of such buildings was ruthlessly implemented in purely functional terms. Spoiling and damaging the original structure and its fittings was accepted without question. For instance, silicate bricks were used for annexes; spatial dimensions were changed by removing walls; and larger rooms were transformed into sports halls. Other manor houses were converted into blocks of flats.

Former owners of such residences were left with little more than memories, a few pieces of furniture, and photos. Some of them attempted to preserve the ambience and lifestyle of what used to be their manors by reconstructing entire interiors within their new dwellings.

◂ Beļava manor (Kortenhof, LV). Since 1926 this country house, which had remained undamaged, has been a primary school. Some decorative elements from the original baroque furnishings – such as stucco on the ceiling, wall-panelling, built-in cupboards, and door ornamentation – have been preserved.

Herrenhaus Degahlen/Degole (LV). Das Schild über dem Haupteingang zum früheren Herrenhaus Degahlen weist das Gebäude als »Propagandazentrum« aus. Eine Tafel mit dem Lob auf die Union der Sozialistischen Sowjet-Republiken am Gesims darüber macht deutlich, dass es sich hierbei um einen Wirkungsort der kommunistischen Machthaber handelt. Foto um 1956

Degole manor (Degahlen, LV). The sign over the main entrance to the former manor house shows that the building became a »Propaganda Centre«. Eulogy of the Union of Soviet Socialist Republics on the cornice above makes clear that this is now a place where the communist authorities are active. Photo about 1956

Herrenhaus Koltzen/Bīriņi (LV). Von 1925 bis 1995 war das einstige Herrenhaus ein Sanatorium, in dem Herz- und Atembeschwerden behandelt wurden. Heute ist das in Privatbesitz geführte Gebäude ein Spa-Hotel und beliebtes Ausflugsziel. Das Foto entstand 1971.

Bīriņi manor (Koltzen, LV). From 1925 to 1995 the former manor house was a sanatorium where people with heart problems and breathing difficulties received treatment. Today the now privately-owned building is a spa-hotel and a popular place for outings. The photo was taken in 1971.

Löwenberg/Lauvaskalns (LV), Speisezimmer im Sommerhaus der Familie von Gersdorff

Lauvaskalns (Löwenberg, LV), dining room in the von Gersdorff family's summer house

Speisezimmer im Privathaus der Familie Solms/Gersdorff in Marburg/Lahn. Die Einrichtung des in den 1930er Jahren erbauten Wohnhauses lehnt sich an die im einstigen Sommersitz auf dem Löwenberg/Lauvaskalns an.

Dining room in the private house of the Solms/Gersdorff family at Marburg/Lahn, built in the 1930s. The furnishings in this dwelling are based on the family's former summer residence on the Lauvaskalns (Löwenberg).

Engagement für den Erhalt
Baltische Herrenhäuser heute

Die aktuelle Situation der Burgen, Schlösser und Herrenhäuser ist in Estland und Lettland ähnlich wie andernorts in Europa auch. Neben einigen Dutzend herausragend rekonstruierten und zumeist als Hotel oder in öffentlicher Nutzung als Kultureinrichtung oder Museum befindlichen Beispielen harrt die Mehrheit der bis heute erhaltenen Baudenkmäler auf ihre Instandsetzung und eine neue, sinnvolle Nutzung. Zudem verloren viele Herrenhäuser ihre Funktion aus der Sowjetzeit, stehen heute leer und verfallen. Doch haben es Architekturforscher und Denkmalpfleger in den letzten knapp drei Jahrzehnten nach der Wiedererlangung der Unabhängigkeit der baltischen Staaten geschafft, die einstige Ablehnung und das Desinteresse in der breiten Öffentlichkeit in Empathie und aktiven Einsatz für den Erhalt dieses kulturellen Erbes umzuwandeln. Immer mehr junge Menschen trauen sich, ein Herrenhaus in mühevoller Eigenarbeit denkmalgerecht wiederherzurichten. Wie einst sind einige von ihnen nun wieder private Wohnhäuser und anziehende Kulturorte. Der Erhalt des reichen architektonischen Erbes der Herrenhäuser und Gutsanlagen in Estland und Lettland bleibt heute und zukünftig eine Herausforderung.

Commitment to Conservation
Baltic Manor Houses Today

In Estonia and Latvia, the current status of castles and manor houses parallels the situation elsewhere in Europe. Apart from several dozen excellently reconstructed buildings mostly used as hotels, cultural institutions, or museums, the majority of such remaining structures still await restoration and renewed, meaningful utilisation. In addition, many manor houses lost their function during the Soviet period and today are empty and run down. Nevertheless, for almost three decades now, following re-establishment of independence for the Baltic states, researchers and conservationists have succeeded in transforming rejection and lack of interest among the general public into support for and active involvement in preservation of this cultural heritage. More and more young people take on the arduous task of appropriate restoration of a manor house. Some of these buildings are once again private dwellings and cultural attractions. However today and for the future maintenance of the rich architectural legacy of manor houses and landed estates in Estonia and Latvia remains a challenge.

◀ Herrenhaus Sack/Saku (EE). Das Gut war im Besitz verschiedener Familien. Paul Eduard Graf Rehbinder (1794–1870) ließ in den 1820er Jahren das Herrenhaus errichten, das zu den schönsten klassizistischen Bauten im Baltikum zählt. Heute befindet sich in dem Gebäude ein Hotel mit Festsälen und Seminarräumen. Karl Friedrich Graf Rehbinder (1764–1841) hatte eine Destillerie und Brauerei gegründet. Saku ist heute die älteste und größte Brauerei in Estland.

◀ Saku manor house (Sack, EE). Over the years this estate was owned by various families. Paul Eduard, Count Rehbinder (1794–1870), had the manor built in the 1820s and this was viewed as being among the most beautiful of such buildings in the Baltic classical style. The manor house has become a hotel with rooms for public events and seminars. Karl Friedrich, Count Rehbinder (1764–1841) founded a distillery and brewery, and Saku is now the oldest and largest brewery in Estonia.

Das Herrenhaus Durben/Durbe (LV) als Museum. In dem klassizistischen Gebäude wird heute dem Besucher die Einrichtung und Lebenswelt in einem deutschbaltischen Herrenhaus aus der Zeit des späten 19. und frühen 20. Jahrhunderts anschaulich vermittelt. Das Haus gehört als Filiale zum Museum in Tuckum/Tukums (LV), eine der führenden Forschungseinrichtungen zur Geschichte und Kultur der Deutschbalten im Baltikum. Das Foto zeigt eine Innenraumeinrichtung mit Möbeln im Stil der Neorenaissance, entstanden zwischen 1869 und 1903.

Durbe manor (Durben, LV) as a museum. In this neoclassical building today's visitors get a vivid idea of the furnishings and life-style of a German Baltic manor house in the late 19th and early 20th centuries. The house is now an outpost of the museum at Tukums (Tuckum), a leading research centre devoted to the history and culture of German Balts. The photo shows the furnishing of an inner room with objects in the Neo-Renaissance style dating from between 1869 and 1903.

Das Herrenhaus Durben/Durbe (LV) wurde vermutlich nach einem Entwurf von Johann Georg Berlitz (1753–1837) im Auftrag von Christoph Johann (Jeannot) Friedrich Reichsgraf von Medem (1763–1838) erbaut. Das hohe und steile Dach deutet daraufhin, dass es sich nicht um einen Neubau, sondern um den Umbau eines bereits vorhandenen Gebäudes handelt.

Durbe manor (Durben, LV). The building was probably based on plans by Johann Georg Berlitz (1753–1837), working for Christoph Johann (Jeannot) Friedrich Reichsgraf (Imperial Count) von Medem (1763–1838). The steep high roof indicates that this was not a new building, but rather a conversion of an already existing construction.

Speisesaal im einstigen Herrenhaus Aß/Kiltsi (EE). Die nach der Aufgabe des Gutes als Folge der Agrarreform im Herrenhaus eingerichtete Schule bewirtschaftet das Gebäude bis heute.

Kiltsi manor (Aß, EE). A school dining room in the former country house. This school, established here after the agricultural reforms, has made use up to the present day of this building.

Herrenhaus Aß/Kiltsi (EE). Im Laufe der Zeit war das Gut im Besitz verschiedener Familien u.a. der Uexkülls, der Benckendorffs und Krusensterns. Das auf einen halbkreisförmigen Grundriss errichtete Herrenhaus wurde von 1784 bis 1790 für Hermann Johann von Benckendorff (1751–1800) auf den Fundamenten einer mittelalterlichen Vasallenburg erbaut. In den 1990er Jahren wurde neben der Schule auch ein Museum zur Erinnerung an den ersten russischen Weltumsegler Adam Johann von Krusenstern (1770–1846) eingerichtet, in dessen Besitz das Gut seit 1816 war.

Residence at Kiltsi (Aß, EE). In the course of time this estate was owned by various families (including the Uexkuells, Benckendorffs, and Krusensterns). The manor house built on a semi-circular site was constructed between 1784 and 1790 for Hermann Johann von Benckendorff (1751–1800) on the foundations of a mediaeval feudal stronghold. In the 1990s a museum was created alongside the school in memory of Adam Johann von Krusenstein (1770–1846) who had owned the estate from 1816 and became famous as the first Russian to sail around the world.

Specification derer unter dem Guthe Salms

befindlichen Bauern, und wie sich selbige nach der gehaltenen Inquisition und Revision in der Hackenzahl angesetzt werden, nemlich

Vorsteher und Bauer Nahmen	Arbeitsahme Mannsleuthe von 15 biß 60 Jahren				Kinder unter 15 Jahren	Alte und Gebrechliche Leuthe	Fremde	
Vom Wesoperra								
Hanso Maddis	1		1		2	2		
Hanso Sönno	1	1	1	2	2			
Atza Sönno	1		1		1			
Reino Jahn	1	1	1		1	4		
Atza Ado	1		1		5			
Usdallo Jahn							1	1
Matzo Jurri						1		
Waino Mart			1			1	1	
Korwekortze Jahn		2	1		1		1	1
Reoja Mick	1		1		2			
Oja Ere Gustav	1		1		2	3		
Transport	7	4	9	2	16	11	4	2

Anhang
Appendix

Ausgewählte Literatur • Selected Bibliography

Ants, Hein: Eesti mõisad/Herrenhäuser in Estland/Estonian Manor Houses 1860–1939. Tallinn 2002

Ants, Hein: Palmse. Palms. Ein Herrenhof in Estland. Tallinn 1996

Bruģis, Dainis: Historisma pilis Latvijā [Schlösser des Historismus in Lettland/Manor Houses of the Historicism Period in Latvia]. Rīga 1997 (m. Zusammenfassung in dt. u. engl. Sprache/with a summary in German and English)

Eesti Mõisad/Herrenhäuser in Estland/Estonian Manor Houses. Koostanud/Zusammengestellt von/Compiled by Ants Hein. Tänapäev 2004

Glanz und Elend. Mythos und Wirklichkeit der Herrenhäuser im Baltikum. Hg. v. Ilse v. zur Mühlen im Auftrag der Carl-Schirren-Gesellschaft e. V. und des Ostpreußischen Landesmuseums. Lüneburg 2012

Gruenewaldt, Anna v.: Erinnerungen. Fellin 1914

Heck, Kilian/**Bock,** Sabine/**Olschewski,** Jana: Schlösser und Herrenhäuser der Ostseeregion. Bausteine einer europäischen Kulturlandschaft. Castles and Manor Houses in the Baltic Sea Region. Components of an European Cultural Heritage. Schwerin 2017

In Gutshäusern und Residenzen. Denkwürdigkeiten der Freifrau Sophie von Hahn. Hg. v. Otto Freiherrn v. Taube. Hannover-Döhren 1964

Lancmanis, Imants: Vidzemes muižu arhitektūra = Architektur Livländischer Gutshäuser. Rundāle 2015

Līne, Ina/**Bruģis,** Dainis: Liecinieki. Latvijas piļu un kungu māju interjeri 19. gadsimtā-20. gadsimta sākumā [Zeugen. Interieurs von Herrenhäusern und Schlössern in Lettland vom 19. bis zum frühen 20. Jahrhundert/Witnesses. Interiors of Manor Houses in Latvia during the 19th to early 20th century]. Tukums 2013 (m. Zusammenfassung in dt. u. engl. Sprache/with a summary in German and English)

Muiža zem Ozoliem. Ungurmuiža un fon Kampenhauzenu dzimta Vidzemē/Gutshof unter den Eichen. Orellen und die Familie von Campenhausen in Livland. Bearb. v. Imants Lancmanis. Ausstellungskat. Rundāles pils muzejs und Herder-Institut, Marburg. Rīga 1998

Ozola, Agrita: Muižu stāsti. Izstādes katalogs [Gütergeschichten. Ausstellungskatalog/Estate Stories, exhibition catalogue]. Tukums 2009 (Text lett., engl. u. dt./text in Latvian, English, and German)

Pirang, Heinz: Baltische Baudenkmäler, Bd. 1: Das baltische Herrenhaus, Teil 1: Die älteste Zeit bis um 1750. Riga 1926

Pirang, Heinz: Baltische Baudenkmäler, Bd. 1: Das baltische Herrenhaus, Teil 2: Die Blütezeit um 1800. Riga 1928

Pirang, Heinz: Baltische Baudenkmäler, Bd. 1: Das baltische Herrenhaus, Teil 3: Die neuere Zeit seit 1850. Riga 1930

Pirang, Heinz: Das baltische Herrenhaus, Nachdruck [d. Ausgabe 1926–1930]. Hannover-Döhren 1976–1979

Raudsepa, Ingrīda/**Upeniece,** Daiga: Paula fon Tranzē-Rozeneka kolekcija/Sammlung Paul von Transehe-Roseneck. Rīga 2005

Thomson, Erik/**Rauch,** Georg von: Schloss Ratshof in Estland. Vom Musenhof zum Nationalmuseum. Lüneburg 1985

Über die Autorin • About the Author

Agnese Bergholde-Wolf, geboren in Cēsis, Lettland, studierte von 2000 bis 2007 Kunstgeschichte, Osteuropäische Geschichte und Baltische Philologie an der Westfälischen Wilhelms-Universität (WWU) Münster. 2008 war sie Mitarbeiterin am Staatlichen Amt für Denkmalpflege Lettlands in Riga. Ende 2011 wurde sie an der Kunstakademie Lettland in Riga promoviert. Seit Oktober 2013 ist sie Mitarbeiterin im Bildarchiv des Herder-Instituts für historische Ostmitteleuropaforschung in Marburg/L. und an diversen Projekten des Instituts beteiligt. Ihre Arbeitsschwerpunkte sind mittelalterliche (Backstein-)Architektur und Bauplastik im Baltikum sowie Architektur und Kunst in Lettland.

Agnese Bergholde-Wolf, born at Cesis in Latvia, studied Art History, Eastern European History, and Baltic Philology from 2000 to 2007 at the Westphalian Wilhelms University (WWU) at Muenster. The following year she worked for the Latvian State Office for Preservation of Historic Monuments. At the end of 2011 she completed a doctorate at the Latvian Art Academy, also in Riga. Since October 2013 she has been on the staff of the image archive of the Herder Institute for Historical Research on East Central Europe, based at Marburg/L. Her work mainly focuses on Baltic mediaeval architecture in brick and its ornamentation, and on architecture and art in Latvia.

Abbildungsnachweis • Illustration Credits

Das Deutsche Kulturforum östliches Europa dankt für die erteilten Reproduktionsgenehmigungen und die freundliche Unterstützung bei der Realisierung dieser Publikation. Das Kulturforum hat sich bis Produktionsschluss intensiv bemüht, alle weiteren Inhaber von Abbildungsrechten ausfindig zu machen. Personen und Institutionen, die möglicherweise nicht erreicht wurden und Rechte an verwendeten Abbildungen beanspruchen, werden gebeten, sich nachträglich mit dem Kulturforum in Verbindung zu setzen.

The German Culture Forum for Central and Eastern Europe wishes to thank all sources of reproduction rights and other generous support during implementation of this publication. The Forum has endeavoured to track down all other individuals and institutions possessing such rights. Persons or institutions holding rights to images used here and possibly not contacted are asked to reply to the Forum.

© Herder-Institut, Marburg. Bildarchiv: 8, 13, 14, 16, 23, 36, 41, 46, 47, 48, 56, 58, 59, 61, 67, 68, 70, 72, 74, 75, 78, 82, 89, 90, 104
Umschlagvorder- und Rückseite sowie Umschlaginnenseite hinten/Front and back covers plus back verso
  Christopher Herrmann: 20 (r.)
  Karl Hintzer: 34, 45, 91
  Vitolds Mašnovskis: 4, 21, 22, 28, 29, 30, 38, 40, 55, 62, 64, 65, 80, 85, 92, 100, 101
  Thomas Helms, Schwerin: 6, 10, 20 (l.), 24, 32, 33, 44, 50, 52, 86, 98, 102

© Herder-Institut, Marburg. Dokumentesammlung/Herder Institute collection of documents:
26, 53, 54, 71: Archiv der Estländischen Ritterschaft/Archive of the Baltic Noble Corporation of Estonia, Bestand DSHI_190_Estland
84, 88: Archiv der Kurländischen Ritterschaft/Archive of the Baltic Noble Corporation of Courland, Bestand DSHI_190_Kurland

66: Ostpreußisches Landesmuseum mit Deutschbaltischer Abteilung/East Prussian state museum with its Baltic German department, Lüneburg/Münnich-Nolcken'scher Familiennachlass/Estate »von Nolden/von Münnich«; 42: Wissenschaftliches Archiv Schlossmuseum Rundāle/Rundāles pils muzejs, Zinātniskais arhīvs/The Scientific Archive at the Rundāle Palace Museum (Lettland/Latvia); 94: Museum Tuckum/Tukuma muzejs/Tukums Museum (Lettland, Latvia); 60: Museum Valmiera/Valmieras Muzejs/Valmiera Museum (Lettland, Latvia); 76, 77: Latvijas Nacionālais vēstures muzejs/Museum der Geschichte Lettlands/National History Museum of Latvia 96, 97: Privatbesitz/private collection
95: © birinupils.lv; 18: © Wikimedia Commons, Ivar Leidus;
35: www.tobyns.com/elley; 103: © Wikimedia Commons, Ren12;
39: www.visitestonia.com/de/das-herrenhaus-alatskivi-dt-allatzkiwwi;
2: © Yegorovnick/Alamy Stock Foto

Folgende Abbildungen wurden den nachstehenden Publikationen entnommen/These illustrations were taken from the following publications:
27: *Muiža zem Ozoliem/Gutshof unter den Eichen*, S./p. 99
83: *Livlands zerstörte Schlösser*. Riga, Leipzig [1906], Bd. III, S./p. 22

Karte Umschlag Innenseite/map front cover verso: Dipl.-Ing. Dirk Bloch, Stadtplanerei BLOCHPLAN, Berlin

Das **Deutsche Kulturforum östliches Europa** engagiert sich für die Vermittlung deutscher Kultur und Geschichte des östlichen Europa. Dabei sind alle Regionen im Blick, in denen Deutsche gelebt haben oder bis heute leben. Das Kulturerbe dieser Gebiete verbindet die Deutschen mit ihren Nachbarn. Das soll einer breiten Öffentlichkeit bewusst gemacht werden – im Dialog und in zukunftsorientierter Zusammenarbeit mit Partnern aus dem östlichen Europa.

Zum Programmangebot des Kulturforums gehören Podiumsgespräche, Vorträge, Thementage, Lesungen, Filmreihen, Wanderausstellungen, Preisverleihungen, Konzerte und Workshops. In seiner **Potsdamer Bibliothek östliches Europa** erscheinen Sachbücher und Kulturreiseführer. Unter www.kulturforum.info, auf der Facebook-Seite, dem Instagram- und dem Youtube-Kanal des Kulturforums können Veranstaltungshinweise, Radio- und Fernsehtipps, Rezensionen, Nachrichten, virtuelle Ausstellungen, Audiomitschnitte und Filme abgerufen werden.

Das Kulturforum versteht sich als Vermittler zwischen Ost und West, zwischen Wissenschaft und Öffentlichkeit, zwischen Institutionen und Einzelinitiativen. Mit seiner Arbeit möchte es einen aktiven Beitrag zu internationaler Verständigung und Versöhnung in Europa leisten.

The **German Culture Forum for Central and Eastern Europe** is committed to forward-looking debate on the history of those areas of Central and Eastern Europe where Germans used to live or still do so. Through dialogue and co-operation with partners in Central and Eastern Europe the Forum aims to present the history of these regions as a common heritage linking Germans and their eastern neighbours, and to make this available to a wide audience.

The Forum organises discussions, lectures, days devoted to specific topics, readings, film series, travelling exhibitions, prize-givings, concerts, and workshops. It publishes popular scholarly work in its **Potsdam Central and Eastern Europe Series.** The website www.kulturforum.info/en, the Facebook Page, the Instagram and the Youtube Channel of the Culture Forum provide information on events, news, reports, documentation, virtual exhibitions, podcasts, and films.

The Forum sees itself as a mediator between East and West, between scholarship and the general public, and between institutions and individuals. Its work makes an active contribution to international understanding and reconciliation in Europe.

Das **Herder-Institut** ist eine zentrale Einrichtung der historischen Ostmitteleuropaforschung in Deutschland. Es beschäftigt sich mit der Geschichte und Kultur Polens, Estlands, Lettlands, Litauens, Tschechiens, der Slowakei und der Region Kaliningrad und bietet eine der besten Spezialbibliotheken mit einer umfangreichen Pressesammlung. Die wissenschaftlichen Sammlungen bestehen aus einem Bildarchiv, einer Kartensammlung und einer Dokumentesammlung mit Baltikum-Schwerpunkt. Das Institut verfügt über eine strukturierte Karriereförderung im Rahmen seiner Herder Institute Research Academy. Ein Stipendienprogramm ermöglicht Forschungsaufenthalte von bis zu drei Monaten. Zu den zahlreichen Veröffentlichungen des Instituts zählen die *Zeitschrift für Ostmitteleuropa-Forschung* sowie diverse Reihen für Studien, Tagungen und Quellenmaterial. Neben einem Bibliografieportal bietet das Institut auch eine Online-Quellenedition mit Texten in Originalsprache und deutscher Übersetzung für die universitäre Lehre an.

Das Herder-Institut betreibt auf der Basis seiner umfangreichen Sammlungen eigene Forschungen, darunter Projekte im Bereich der Geschichte, der sammlungsbezogenen Kulturwissenschaften und der Konzipierung und Implementierung multimedialer Wissensportale. Das Herder-Institut beteiligt sich an der Ständigen Kommission für wissenschaftliche Infrastruktureinrichtungen und Forschungsmuseen sowie an Forschungsverbünden der Leibniz-Gemeinschaft und unterstützt deren Karrierestrategien.

The **Herder Institute** is one of the central facilities of historical East Central European research in Germany. It focuses on the history and culture of Poland, Estonia, Latvia, Lithuania, the Czech Republic, Slovakia and the Kaliningrad region and offers one of the best specialist libraries and maintains extensive collections (images, maps, archival materials on the Baltic States). It conducts research and development projects, organises conferences and workshops. The Herder Institute Research Academy (HIRA) offers a structured training and a lively ex-change with researchers who are working on similar topics. The HIRA provides a forum for young researchers to draw up academic theses. A fellowship-program enables researchers to conduct research up to three months. The publications of the institute's own publishing department include also the *Journal of East Central European Studies (Zeitschrift für Ostmitteleuropa-Forschung).* The Institute offers an online bibliographic service and a portal on the history of East Central Europe for university teaching purposes.

The Herder Institute conducts its own research based on its large collection, including projects in history, collection-based cultural studies, and the conception and implementation of a multimedia knowledge portal. The Herder Institute is one of the institutions and research museums participating in the Permanent Commission for Scientific Infrastructure as well as in the research associations of the Leibniz Association, and it supports the career strategies of these organisations.

Umschlagvorderseite: Kuppel im Festsaal von Schloss Mesothen/Mežotne (LV, s. a. S. 30 f.)
Front cover: Cupola in the grand hall of Mežotne residence (Mesothen, LV, see also pp. 30 f.)
Umschlaginnenseite vorne: Karte der russischen Ostseeprovinzen mit den im Katalog vorgestellten Herrenhäusern
Front cover verso: Map of Russian Baltic provinces with manor houses presented in the catalogue
Umschlaginnenseite hinten: Herrenhaus Katzdangen/Kazdanga (LV, s. a. S. 80 ff.), Gartenseite
Back cover verso: Kazdanga (Katzdangen, LV, see also pp. 80 ff.), residence from the garden
Umschlagrückseite: Detail einer Innenaufnahme in Schloss Ratshof/Raadi (EE, s. a. S. 34)
Back cover: Interior detail of Raadi residence (Ratshof, EE, see also p. 34)
S. 16: Palms/Palmse (EE, s. a. S. 25 f.), Stahlstich von W. Knopfmacher nach Wilhelm Siegfried Stavenhagen
p. 16: Palmse (Palms, EE, see also pp. 25 f.), steel engraving by W. Knopfmacher after Wilhelm Siegfried Stavenhagen
S. 48: Gut Elley/Eleja (LV, s. a. S. 31), Gemälde, 19. Jahrhundert • p. 48: The Estate Eleja (Elley, LV, see also p. 31), painting, 19th century
S. 78: Wappenrelief auf dem ehemaligen Gut Kabillen/Kabile (LV, s. a. S. 22)
p. 78: Relief coat of arms at the former Kabile estate (Kabillen, LV, see also p. 22)
S. 104: Aufgeschlagenes Wackenbuch des Gutes Palms (siehe S. 71) • p. 104: Open work-book, called *Wackenbuch* from the Palmse estate (see p. 71)

2., durchgesehene Auflage 2020
© 2020 Deutsches Kulturforum östliches Europa e. V.
Berliner Straße 135
D-14467 Potsdam
www.kulturforum.info

Gefördert von/Supported by:

Alle Rechte vorbehalten/All rights reserved.
Allen, die am Zustandekommen dieses Buches in vielfältiger Weise beteiligt waren, sei an dieser Stelle herzlich gedankt.
With thanks to all those who contributed in many different ways to the creation of this book.

Konzeption und Text • concept and text: Agnese Bergholde-Wolf
Redaktion • editing: Claudia Tutsch
Übersetzung ins Englische • translation into English: Tim Nevill
Layout: Anna Dejewska-Herzberg
Druck • printing: Brandenburgische Universitätsdruckerei, Potsdam

Die zweisprachige Wanderausstellung *Adeliges Leben im Baltikum. Herrenhäuser in Estland und Lettland* wurde vom Deutschen Kulturforum östliches Europa Potsdam in Kooperation mit dem Herder-Institut für historische Ostmitteleuropaforschung – Institut der Leibniz-Gemeinschaft, Marburg/L., erstellt.
The bilingual travelling exhibition *The Life of the Baltic Nobility. Manor Houses in Estonia and Latvia* was put together by the German Culture Forum for Central and Eastern Europe Potsdam, in co-operation with the Herder Institute for Historical Research on East Central Europe – Institute of the Leibniz Association, Marburg/L.

Diese Ausgabe wurde auf chlor- und säurefrei gebleichtem, alterungsbeständigem Papier gedruckt.
This book complies with the environmental and technological requirements of long-lasting paper.
Printed in Germany.

ISBN 978-3-936168-87-7

Innovation und Tradition
Hinrich Brunsberg und die spätgotische Backsteinarchitektur in Pommern und der Mark Brandenburg

Hinrich Brunsberg (um 1350 bis nach 1428) ist neben den Parlern einer der bedeutendsten und auf dem Gebiet der Backsteinarchitektur einer der wenigen namentlich bekannten mittelalterlichen Baumeister im südlichen Ostseeraum. Das Buch stellt die mit seinem Namen verbundenen Kirchen, Rathäuser und Stadttore in Pommern und der Mark Brandenburg vor. Sie zeichnen sich durch moderne Technologie und vielgestaltige Schmuckelemente aus, wie anhand der zahlreichen aktuellen und historischen Fotografien deutlich wird. Erstmals greifbar wird Brunsbergs charakteristisches Dekor aus aufwendigen Formsteinprofilen, feingliedrigen Maßwerkfüllungen und Ziergiebeln am Chor der Marienkirche in Stargard/Stargard Szczeciński. Texte ausgewiesener Fachleute informieren über die mit Brunsberg verbundenen Bauwerke, Strömungen in der Architektur an der Schwelle der Spätgotik zur Frührenaissance sowie über die Geschichte Pommerns und der Mark Brandenburg in dieser Zeit.

Eine ins Polnische übersetzte Ausgabe ist beim historisch-kulturellen Verein »Terra Incognita«, Königsberg i. d. Neumark/Chojna, erschienen.

Mit Fotografien von Thomas Voßbeck
u. zahlr. farb. u. S.-W.-Fotos
120 S., Broschur
€ [D] 9,80/€ [A] 10,–
ISBN 978-3-936168-60-0
Mit Beiträgen von Ernst Badstübner, Jarosław Jarzewicz, Barbara Ochendowska-Grzelak, Wolfgang Ribbe und Dirk Schumann